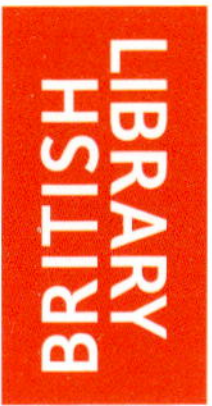

PAINTED LABYRINTH

The world of the Lindisfarne Gospels

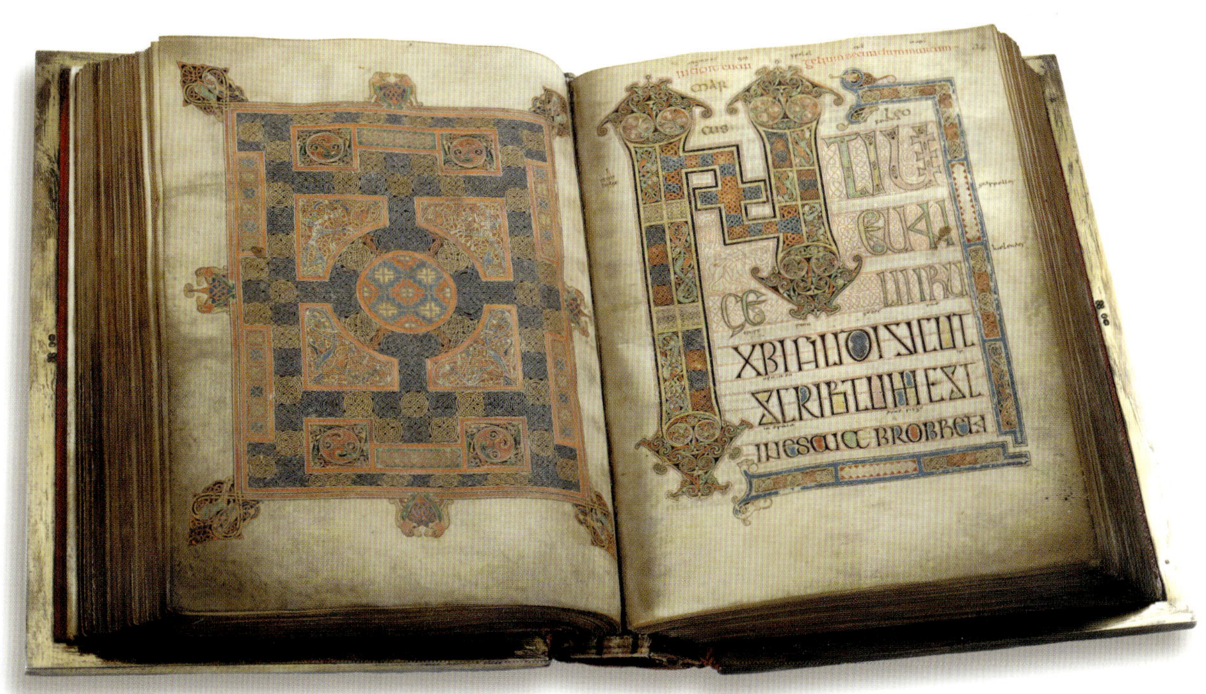

Michelle P. Brown

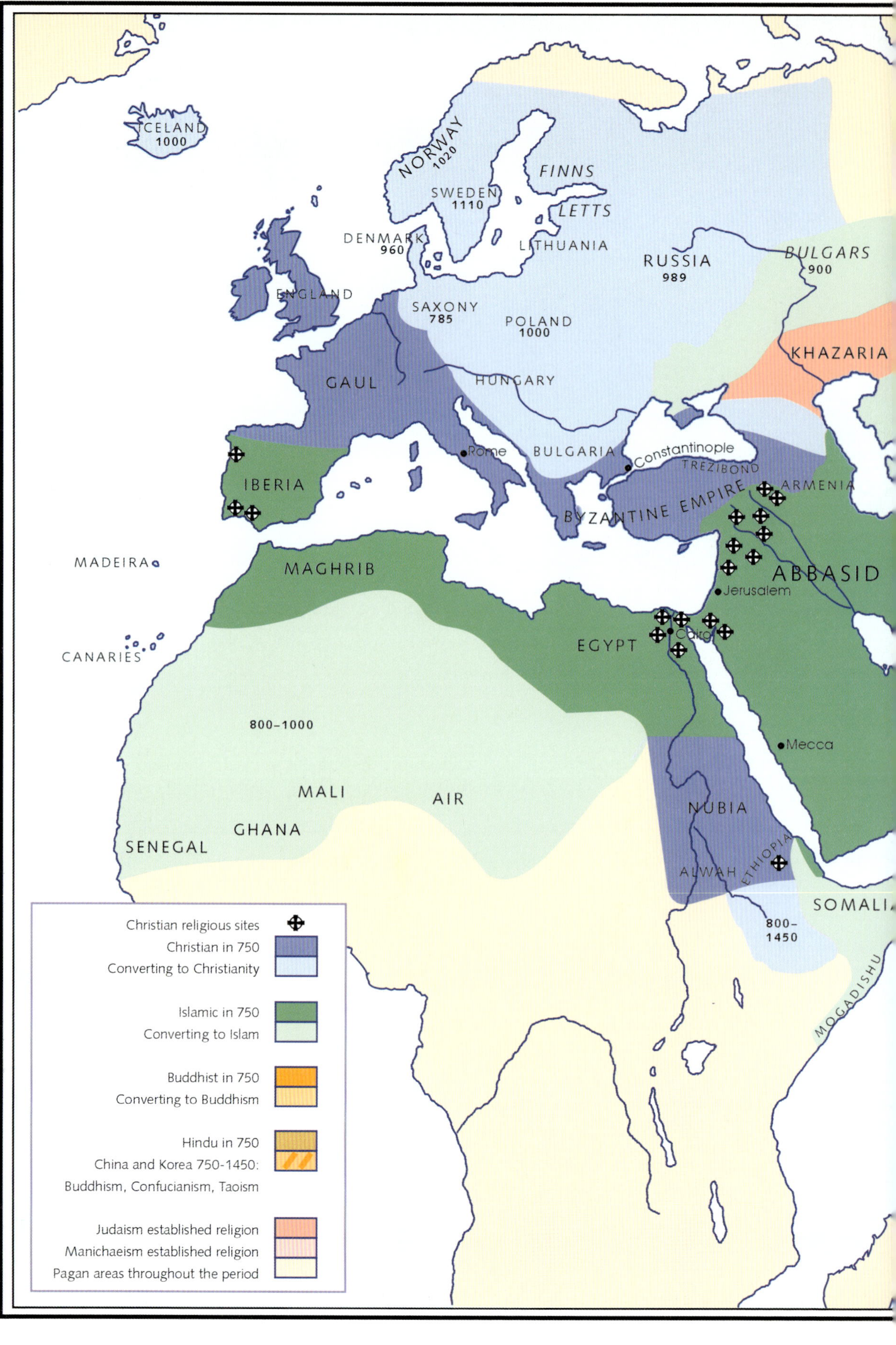
ICELAND
1000
NORWAY
1020
SWEDEN
1110
FINNS
LETTS
DENMARK
960
LITHUANIA
RUSSIA
989
BULGARS
900
ENGLAND
SAXONY
785
POLAND
1000
KHAZARIA
GAUL
HUNGARY
Rome
BULGARIA
Constantinople
TREZIBOND
BYZANTINE EMPIRE
ARMENIA
IBERIA
ABBASID
MADEIRA
MAGHRIB
Jerusalem
CANARIES
EGYPT
Cairo
800–1000
Mecca
MALI
AIR
NUBIA
GHANA
ETHIOPIA
SENEGAL
ALWAH
SOMALI
800–
1450
MOGADISHU
Christian religious sites
Christian in 750
Converting to Christianity
Islamic in 750
Converting to Islam
Buddhist in 750
Converting to Buddhism
Hindu in 750
China and Korea 750-1450:
Buddhism, Confucianism, Taoism
Judaism established religion
Manichaeism established religion
Pagan areas throughout the period

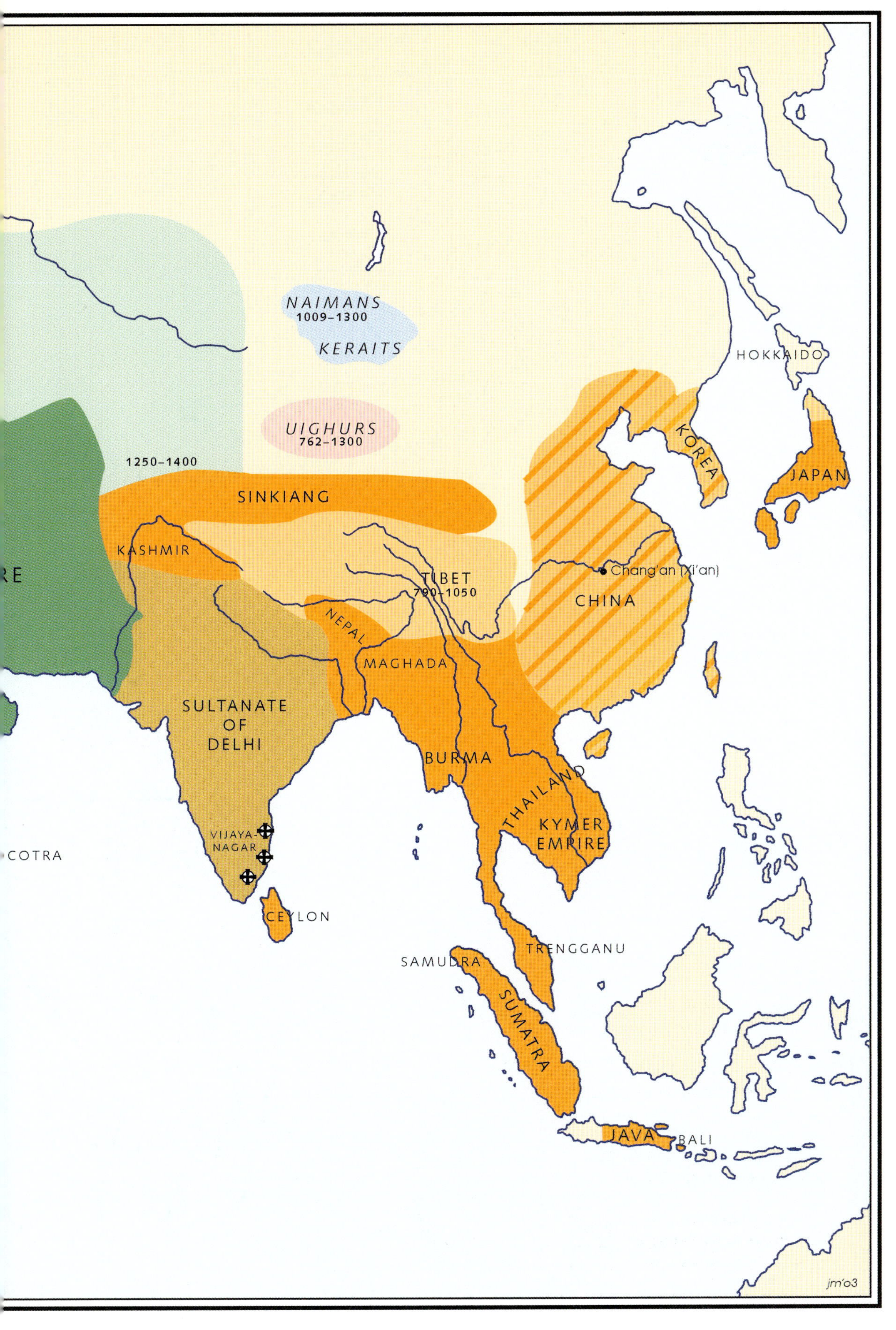

NAIMANS
1009–1300
KERAITS
HOKKAIDO
UIGHURS
762–1300
KOREA
JAPAN
1250–1400
SINKIANG
KASHMIR
Chang'an (Xi'an)
TIBET
790–1050
CHINA
NEPAL
MAGHADA
SULTANATE
OF
DELHI
BURMA
THAILAND
KYMER
EMPIRE
COTRA
VIJAYA-
NAGAR
CEYLON
TRENGGANU
SAMUDRA
SUMATRA
JAVA
BALI
jm'03

INTRODUCTION

The Lindisfarne Gospels form one of the world's great books – a breathtaking artwork and symbol of faith that represents the attempt of a gifted individual to express a whole society's identity and belief, with an energy and passion that still inspire.

The book is thought to have been made around 715-20 in the island monastery of Lindisfarne (Holy Island), in the Anglo-Saxon kingdom of Northumbria in north eastern England, during one of the world's influential periods of transition – from Graeco-Roman Antiquity to the Middle Ages. It reflects Lindisfarne's formative influences:

- the Irish monks from St Columba's island monastery of Iona in Scotland who founded the monastery at Lindisfarne in 635

- the native British peoples left in the wake of the Roman Empire

- the Germanic warlords and settlers who forged the kingdoms that came to form England

- the legacy of Rome and its Early Christian popes and missionaries

- the exotic, timeless mysticism of Byzantium, northern Africa and the Middle East

During the early 8th century, Britain was home to a diverse, multi-cultural community and was establishing a distinctive identity upon the international stage. Out of this meeting of cultures emerged a vigorous new form of learning, literature and art known as 'Insular' ('of the islands' of Britain and Ireland). The Lindisfarne Gospels are one of its most beautiful creations.

Spiritual ideals, political realities and the challenges facing humanity and the environment merge in the Lindisfarne Gospels to form a complex web of words and images – a painted labyrinth of prayer and praise.

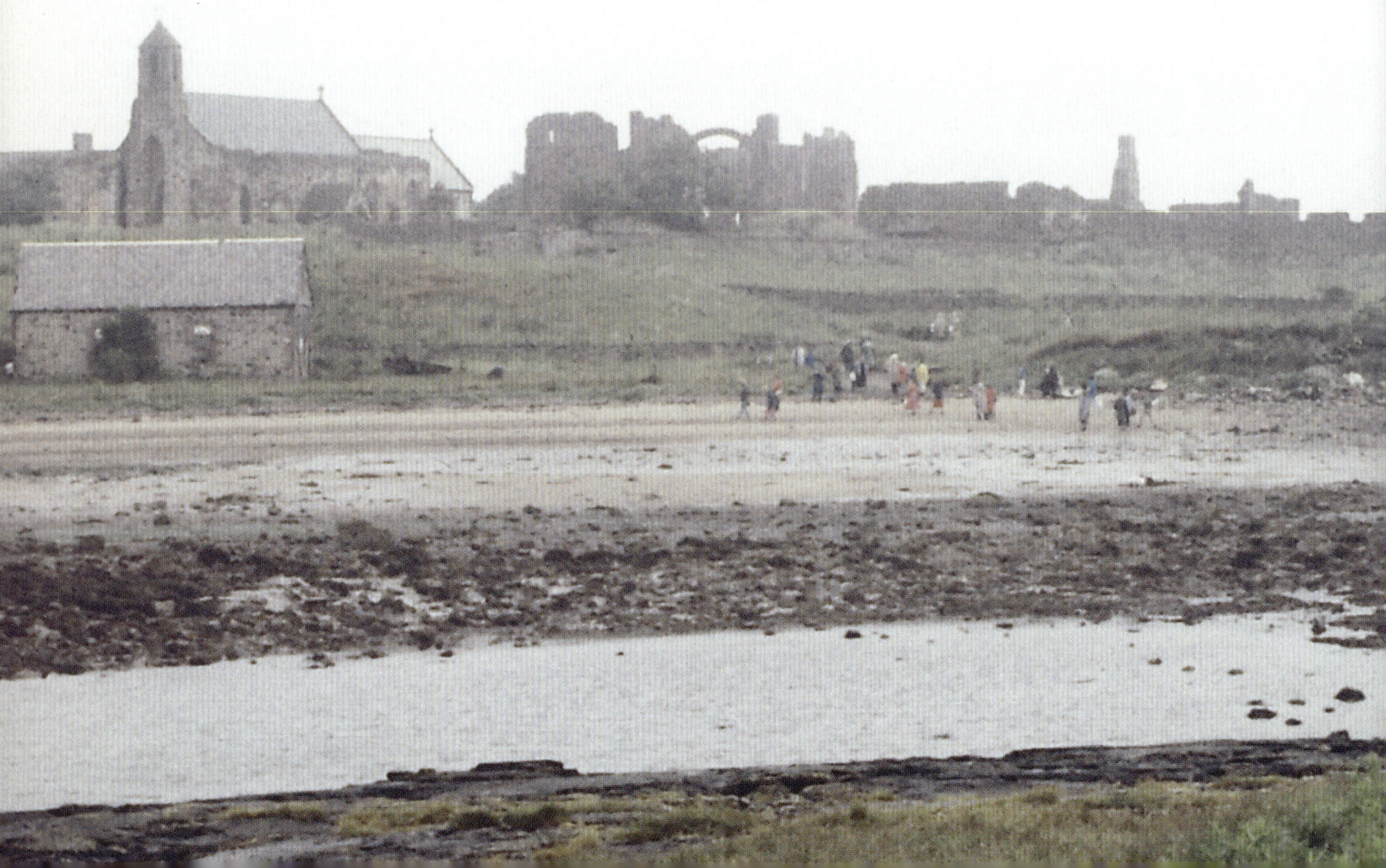

The Background: the World and Faith around 700

The ancient Roman Empire stretched from Britain and the Rhine-Danube frontier to North Africa, Turkey, Palestine and Syria. During the 4th century Christianity became its official religion. During the 5th century the Empire collapsed under its own weight and the influx of peoples from outside who wanted to enjoy its benefits or seize its wealth.

Pagan peoples raided, invaded, settled and formed new kingdoms: the Ostrogoths and Lombards in Italy; the Franks in Gaul; the Visigoths in Spain and Portugal; and the Anglo-Saxons in England. They ruled and mixed with the local populations and were gradually converted to Christianity.

The Romans' eastern Empire continued under the Byzantine emperors based in Constantinople (Istanbul), and the Christian Church under a number of Patriarchs. Rome remained a focus in the West as seat of the Pope, head of the western Church.

During the 7th century, conquests carried Islam around the eastern and southern shores of the Mediterranean and into Spain, but Judaism and Christianity continued to enjoy a measure of toleration there. Other ancient religions – Buddhism, Hinduism, Confucianism, Taoism and Zoroastrianism – were already established further east and likewise spread and interacted.

Further pagan incursions beset Europe: Slavs and Avars from eastern Europe and beyond and, from around 800, the seaborne raiders known as Vikings invaded from Scandinavia. On Christmas Day 800 the Frankish ruler, Charlemagne, was crowned Emperor in Rome by the Pope, establishing a new Christian empire in the West.

Site of the Lindisfarne monastery (with ruined Norman Priory and parish church), seen from St Cuthbert's Isle, an offshore retreat.

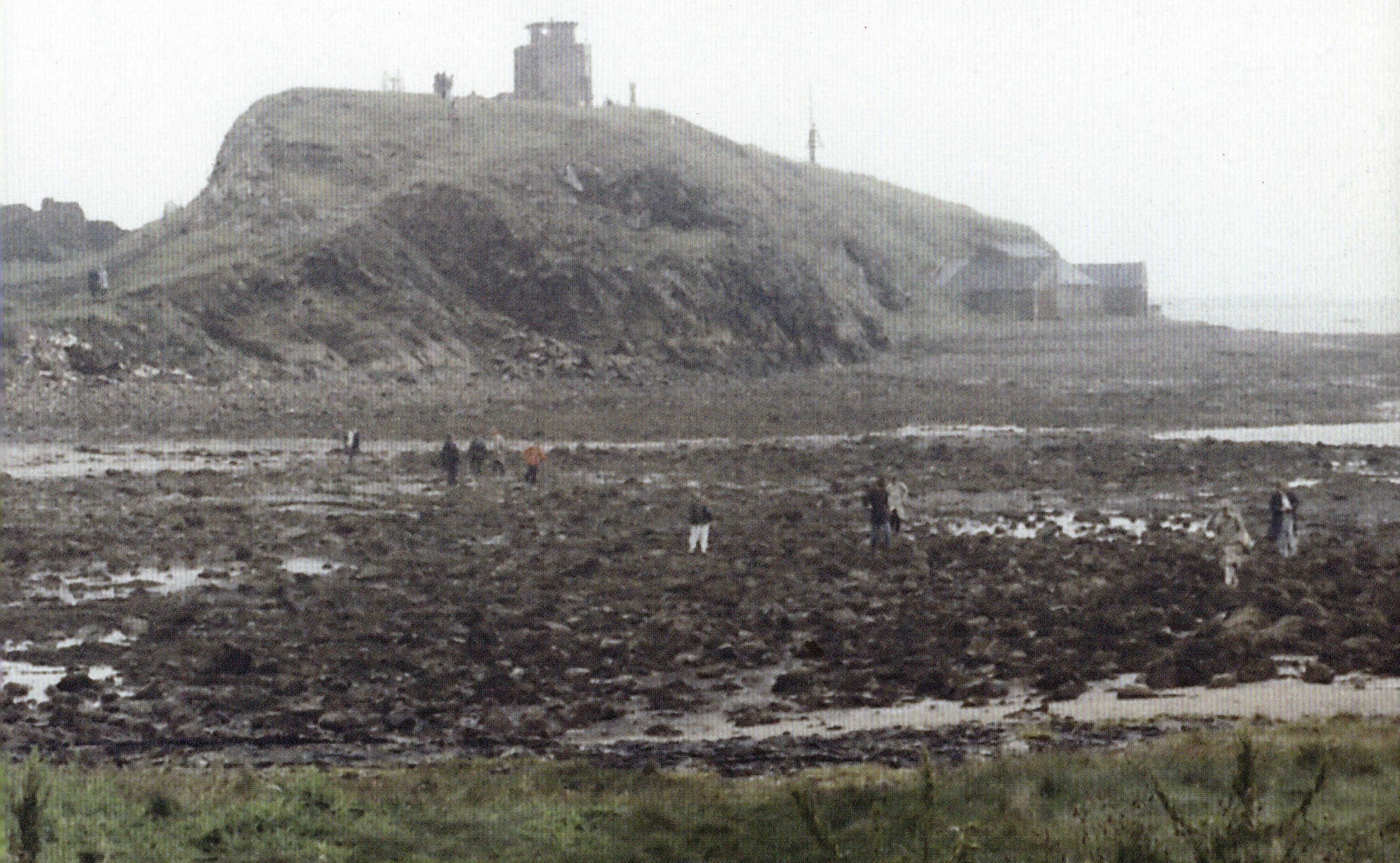

MAKERS AND OWNERS OF THE LINDISFARNE GOSPELS

Britain and Ireland in the Age of Bede

In 597 St Augustine arrived at the court of the pagan King Ethelbert of Kent, having been sent by Pope Gregory the Great to convert the Germanic peoples (Anglo-Saxons) who had taken over the southern and eastern parts of Britain after the Roman Empire collapsed in the early 5th century. That same year the Irish prince-abbot, St Columba, died at his island monastery of Iona (in the kingdom of Dalriada in what is now Argyll). He had founded the centre in 563 as the base for the conversion of Irish settlers in western Scotland, and of the ancient peoples known as Picts who inhabited Scotland, some of whom had been converted earlier by the Britons St Ninian of Whithorn and St Mungo of Glasgow. The Irish settlers were known as 'Scotti' (Irish) and over time came to inter-marry with the Pictish royalty and to rule the region, giving it their name. Columba's family of monasteries eventually came to include Derry, Durrow and Kells in Ireland, Iona and Lindisfarne (with its own foundations, such as Melrose, Jedburgh, Hartlepool, Lichfield and Bradwell-on-Sea in Essex).

This two-pronged 'Roman'/'Celtic' movement by the followers of Saints Augustine and Columba to convert the Anglo-Saxons has tended to be over-simplified in scholarship. Christianity had in fact been introduced to Celtic Britain under the Roman Empire and many Christian British kingdoms survived the Roman withdrawal and Germanic takeover for some time. These included Strathclyde (around Glasgow), the Goddodin around Edinburgh, Rheged (in southern Scotland and Cumbria), Elmet and Lindsey (in the East Midlands), as well as Wales, Cornwall and parts of Pictland. British bishops continued to care for their native flocks, but often avoided contact with their pagan Germanic neighbours. Frankish bishops from Gaul also participated in converting the Anglo-Saxons.

Augustine's mission targeted political court conversions, its missionaries entering via mixed-faith households. King Ethelbert of Kent and King Edwin of Northumbria had both married Christian wives and Augustine's follower, Paulinus, was sent to Edwin's court. Edwin converted and became famed for good government and the stability of his rule. The monk and historian Bede (673-735) says

Left **The Mark 'incipit' page in a 7th-century Gospelbook, probably from Northumbria, with an early instance of an initial with Germanic-style animal ornament. This is an example of the sort of Insular Gospelbook made before the Lindisfarne Gospels. (The Dean and Chapter of Durham Cathedral, Durham MS A.ii.10, f. 2r)**

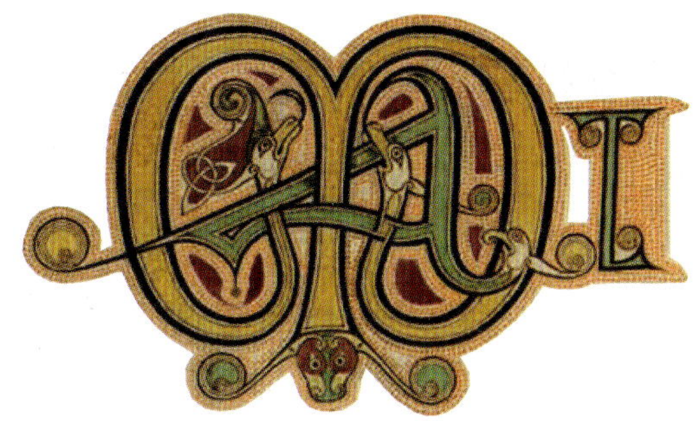

that a woman with a babe in arms could travel unmolested from one side of his kingdom to the other and that drinking fountains were set up along highways. Edwin fell in battle around 632. Paulinus' mission cannot have gained much ground, for he and the royal family then fled to Kent and it was left to Edwin's successor, Oswald, a member of a rival dynasty who had been in exile amongst the Irish of Dalriada, to invite monks from Iona to establish the monastery of Lindisfarne in 635 and to convert Northumbria's people, not just its royal household.

The 'Roman' and 'Celtic' Churches, or more specifically the Columban Church (the centres founded by St Columba and his followers, for many other churches in Ireland already followed Roman practice), observed different traditions. These included alternative methods of calculating the date of Easter as well as physical appearances – Roman clerics had a circular tonsure, or shaved patch, on the top of their heads and Celts a shaved tonsure running across the head from ear to ear with a mane of hair behind.

In 664 a Synod was held at St Hild's monastery of Whitby to settle any dispute between the two. The Columban cause was argued by Bishop Colman of Lindisfarne, and the Roman by the promising young priest, Wilfrid. King Oswy of Northumbria (who had succeeded his brother, Oswald) decided in favour of Rome, for St Peter, its patron, held the keys to heaven and was more powerful. Uniformity was important for a young Church and schism was to be avoided. There were also trade implications. The decision was essentially for Britain to embrace the European mainstream.

Following the decision, some disgruntled Columban clergy left for Ireland, but within a generation the rest of the Irish Church, including Columban centres, had conformed (Iona being the last to comply, in 716). In Northumbria the great rallying point for reconciliation became a charismatic figure bridging both traditions – St Cuthbert.

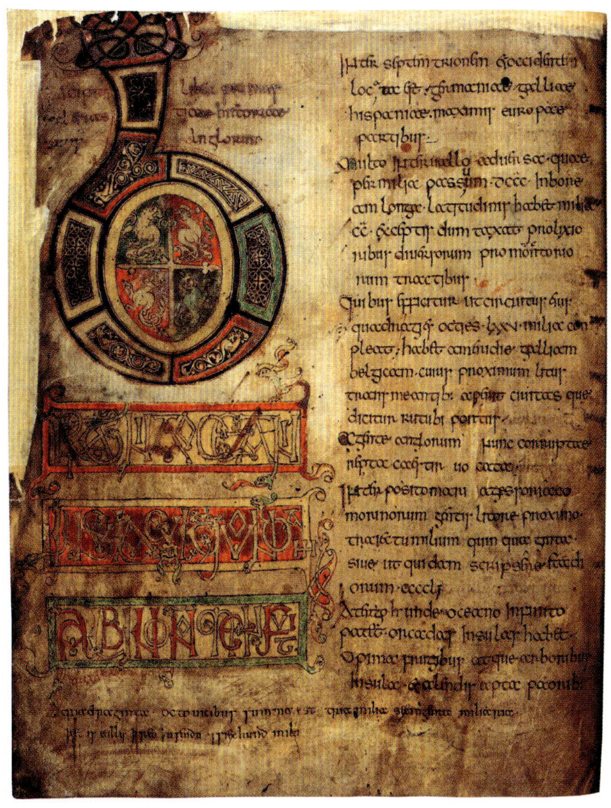

Above **The Wilton Cross, Anglo-Saxon, early 7th century. An early Christian coin has been reset into a pendant during the conversion period, showing the impact of Christian symbols on early Anglo-Saxon art. (The British Museum, MME 1859,5-12,1)**

Above right **The letters 'MAT' from the Lindisfarne Gospels, in which the earlier stylised Germanic animal art becomes more lively and natural in response to Mediterranean models.**

Right **The opening of Book I of Bede's *Ecclesiastical History of the English People*. The Tiberius Bede, Mercia or Kent (Canterbury?), c.825. (The British Library, Cotton MS Tiberius C.ii, f. 5v)**

In 731 Bede completed his *Ecclesiastical History of the English People*, one of our best sources for knowledge of the period and a medieval 'best-seller'. He entered the twin monasteries of (Monk) Wearmouth and Jarrow as a child and only left the cloister on a few local trips, but his grasp of national and international affairs was great and he harvested information from sources as diverse as the nuns of Barking and the papal archives in Rome.

Bede sought in his *History* to bring a sense of identity and cohesion to this new Christian nation which at the time consisted of a fragmented patchwork of territories. In so doing he acknowledged something of the roles played by other cultures in the formation of 'England'. The Lindisfarne Gospels are, in one sense, the visual equivalent of Bede's *History*, celebrating the cultural and ethnic diversity of these islands and their

contacts, and signalling that there was a place for everyone within the new order.

Nationalism has tinged study of the period, the pendulum swinging between an Irish or English origin for Insular art. Recent scholarship perceives a more collaborative approach in which artistic styles and models circulated throughout much of Britain, Ireland and areas of Irish and Anglo-Saxon missionary work on the Continent. Recent archaeological discoveries, including manufacturing debris on sites such as Dunadd (the capital of Dalriada in Argyll), the Mote of Mark (a British fort in Dumfries and Galloway) and Lagore Crannog (in Ireland) have confirmed that the Germanic fashions – such as those from the famous Sutton Hoo treasure, found in an early 7th-century Anglo-Saxon ship-burial in Suffolk – also permeated Celtic regions, while Celtic 'spiralwork' could be found in England and in Insular monasteries in Frisia, Gaul and northern Italy.

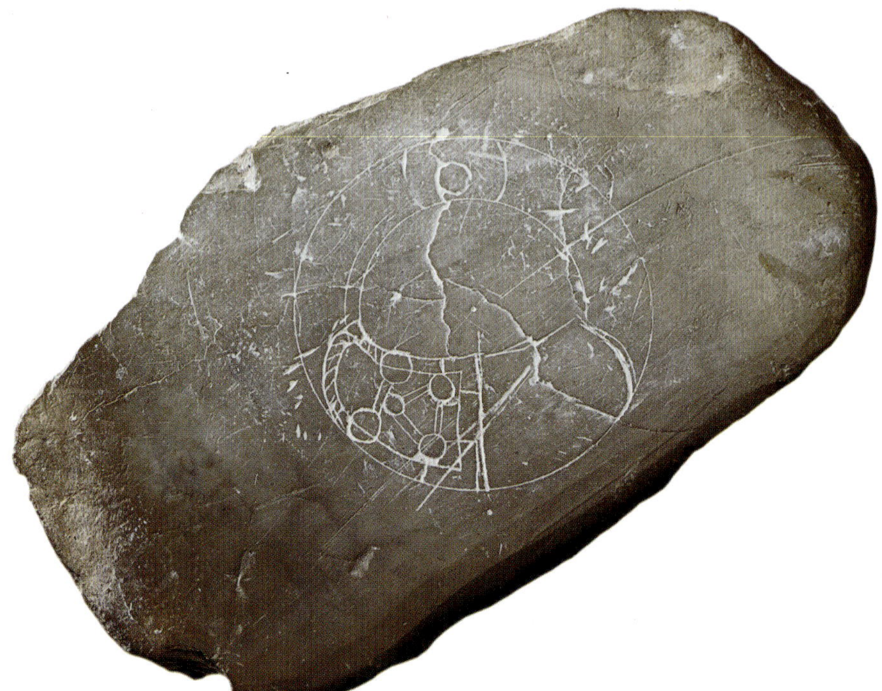

Above A Sutton Hoo shoulder clasp, based on Roman parade armour, with a mount from horse trappings, found during more recent excavations at Sutton Hoo. Anglo-Saxon, early 7th century. (The British Museum, MME 1939, 10-10, 4,5 and Inv. 25a)

Left Stone motif-piece with design for a brooch, from the Irish ceremonial site of Dunadd, Dalriada, Argyll, 8th-9th century. Such manufacturing debris has helped to show that the Insular style and its various ingredients circulated widely throughout Britain and Ireland. (RMS GP 218, Trustees of the National Museums of Scotland)

Rebuilding Rome in Britain

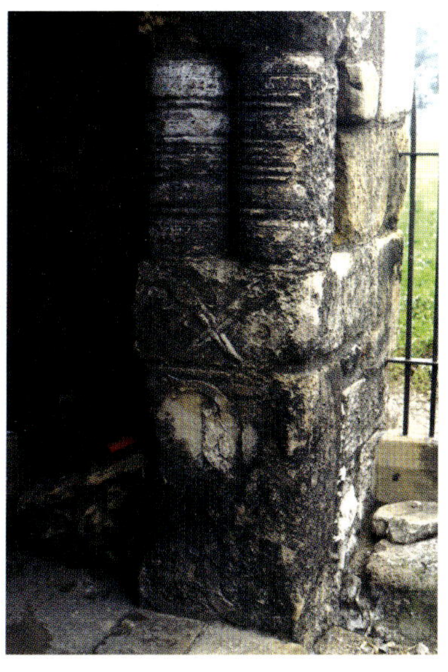

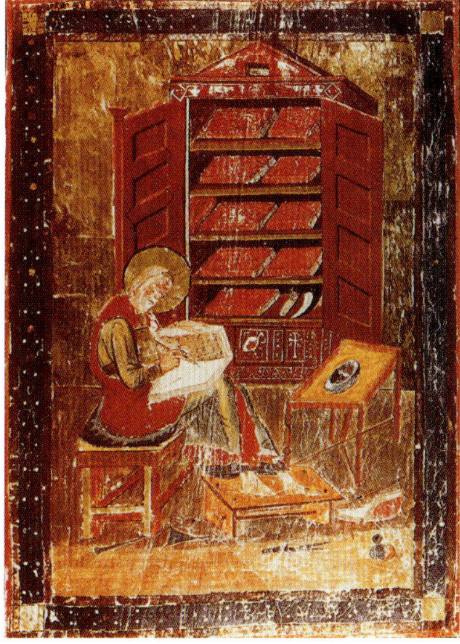

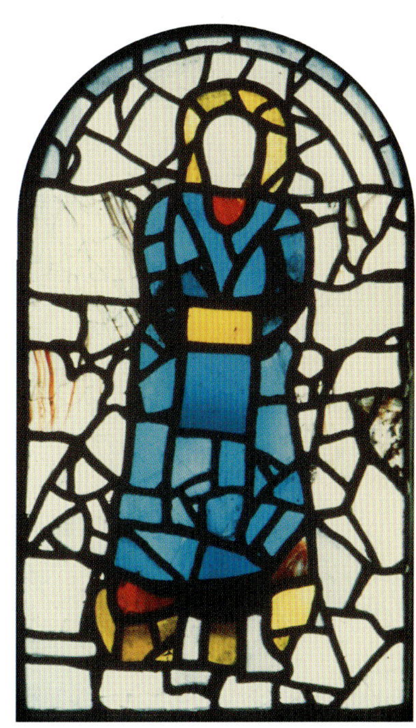

In 667 a new Archbishop of Canterbury was appointed – Theodore of Tarsus (Turkey). He and Hadrian, Abbot of St Augustine's Canterbury (who came from northern Africa, latterly via Naples), established a school of learning that was the envy of Europe, producing scholars such as Aldhelm and (at a distance) Bede. Among Theodore's protégés were the Northumbrian nobles turned clerics, Benedict Biscop, Ceolfrith and Wilfrid. They were filled with an ardour for Rome, Benedict visiting it five times. They brought back books, icons, paintings and other objects, as well as stonemasons and glaziers from Gaul, to adorn their churches which would have been colourful and exotic – these included Biscop's (Monk) Wearmouth and Jarrow, founded in 674 and 681, and Wilfrid's Ripon and Hexham, famed as the largest church north of the Alps. The papal choirmaster, John the Archcantor, came to Northumbria to teach liturgy and chant (and to ensure religious conformity).

Wilfrid's autocratic manner and wealthy churches provoked discord, causing his deposition. (He even governed Lindisfarne for a short, turbulent period after Cuthbert's death in 687.) His travels to Rome to seek papal intervention led to his temporary reinstallation, but dispute continued. England needed some powerful 'PR' if the progress of the previous hundred years was not to be damaged. In 716 an elderly Abbot Ceolfrith left Jarrow for Rome, taking with him one of three complete Bibles he had commissioned from the Wearmouth/Jarrow scriptorium (the 'writing office' of the monastery). Ceolfrith died en route, but his Bible reached the Pope, acting in itself as an ambassador of the English nation. Britain was no provincial outpost, but a leading light. The apostolic mission had made it to the farthest corners of the known world and was reflected back to its centre. That Bible still survives (the Codex Amiatinus in Florence) and was only recognised as an English, rather than an Italo-Byzantine, work about a century ago.

Above left **St Peter's, Monkwearmouth, porch with turned balusters and carved animal ornament by Gaulish masons, 674. (Photo, the author)**

Above centre **The Codex Amiatinus. The Ezra miniature, depicting him writing down the Hebrew Old Testament (which had been lost to fire). This is one of the Bibles commissioned by Abbot Ceolfrith from the Wearmouth/Jarrow scriptorium, before 716. (Florence, Biblioteca Medicea-Laurenziana, MS Amiatino 1, f. V)**

Above right **Stained-glass window, reconstructed as an evangelist figure, from the original easternmost church at Jarrow, 681. (Trustees of Bede's World and the Rector and Churchwardens of St Paul's, Jarrow)**

The Lindisfarne Context

Lindisfarne would have been the ideal place for the blending of cultures seen in the Lindisfarne Gospels. The community was wealthy enough to undertake the project and it needed a magnificent Gospelbook as part of Cuthbert's cult. The hermit-like one-person work and much of the art suggests a 'Celtic' background, the Irish Church having a particular taste for emulating the 'eremitic' traditions of the early monks of the eastern and Egyptian deserts who could live like hermits but still be part of monastic communities, rather than living communally which was the norm in Western monasticism. However, the text and its liturgical associations point to connections with the 'romanising' Wearmouth/Jarrow, centres with which Bishop Eadfrith of Lindisfarne (698-721), the probable artist-scribe of the Lindisfarne Gospels, is known to have been in touch.

It has been thought that the Lindisfarne Gospels were made before Eadfrith assumed the busy role of bishop in 698, ready for the 'translation' (or relocation) of St Cuthbert's remains, but this event was not elaborately pre-planned to accommodate the lengthy work required to make the Lindisfarne Gospels. Cuthbert's grave was opened during Lent and the miraculous surprise of his body's survival, undecayed, had to be related to the Bishop who was in retreat – hardly a major planned event. The growth of Cuthbert's cult c.710-725 provides a better historical context for the manufacture of the Lindisfarne Gospels and the bringing together of their various influences, and this fits better with their stylistic relationship to other artefacts.

Initials in the Lindisfarne Gospels which mark readings only introduced into the Roman liturgy in 715 also point to a later date for their production. If Eadfrith was the artist-scribe he may have begun the work around 715 and been prevented from finishing it by his death in 721. Eadfrith built up Cuthbert's cult after 698. He commissioned a *Life of St Cuthbert* from an anonymous Lindisfarne monk and then a reworking by Bede, who produced an epic verse version and a prose *Life* (completed around 721 and, significantly, dedicated to Eadfrith). Bede's *History* was dedicated to King Ceolwulf of Northumbria who joined the Lindisfarne community and was probably already living there in 731 when Bede's text was finished and presented to him. Lindisfarne was apparently actively collaborating with Wearmouth/Jarrow and may have borrowed a prized Italian Gospelbook from their library as a text model. Bede's influence can be detected in the symbolic imagery of the evangelist miniatures, and the Lindisfarne Gospels' harmonious blending of cultures would fit the image promoted by those working together to create a new collaborative Christian identity for these islands, such as Eadfrith, Bede and Abbot Adomnán of Iona.

Early manuscripts only occasionally contain definite proof of when and where they were made, or by whom, and there is the added complication that they have often travelled away from their places of origin. Scholars have to weigh up the evidence by analysing their style and contents and assessing their relationships with other books and artefacts, some of which (especially sculptures) may have remained in their original place of production.

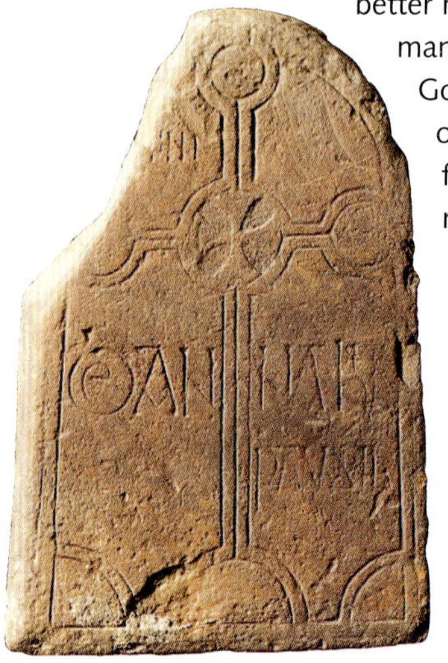

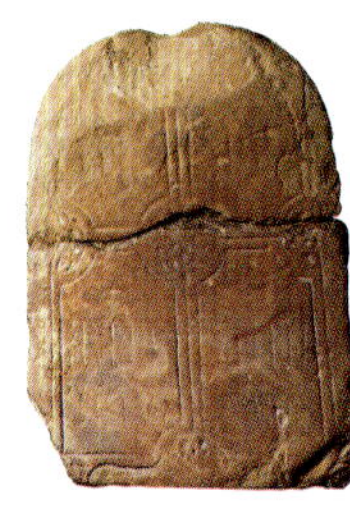

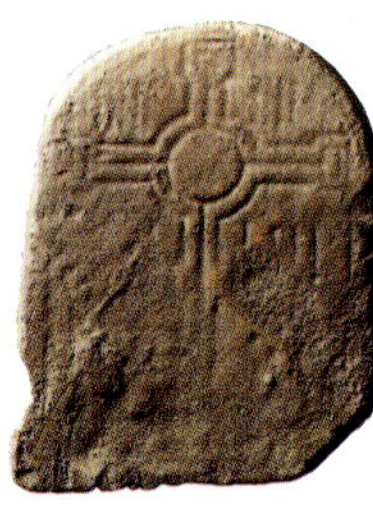

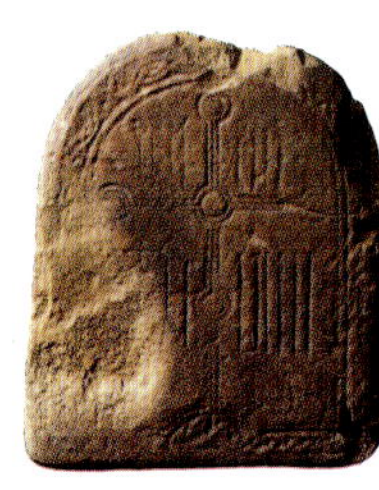

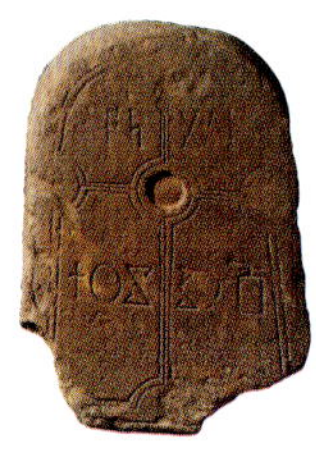

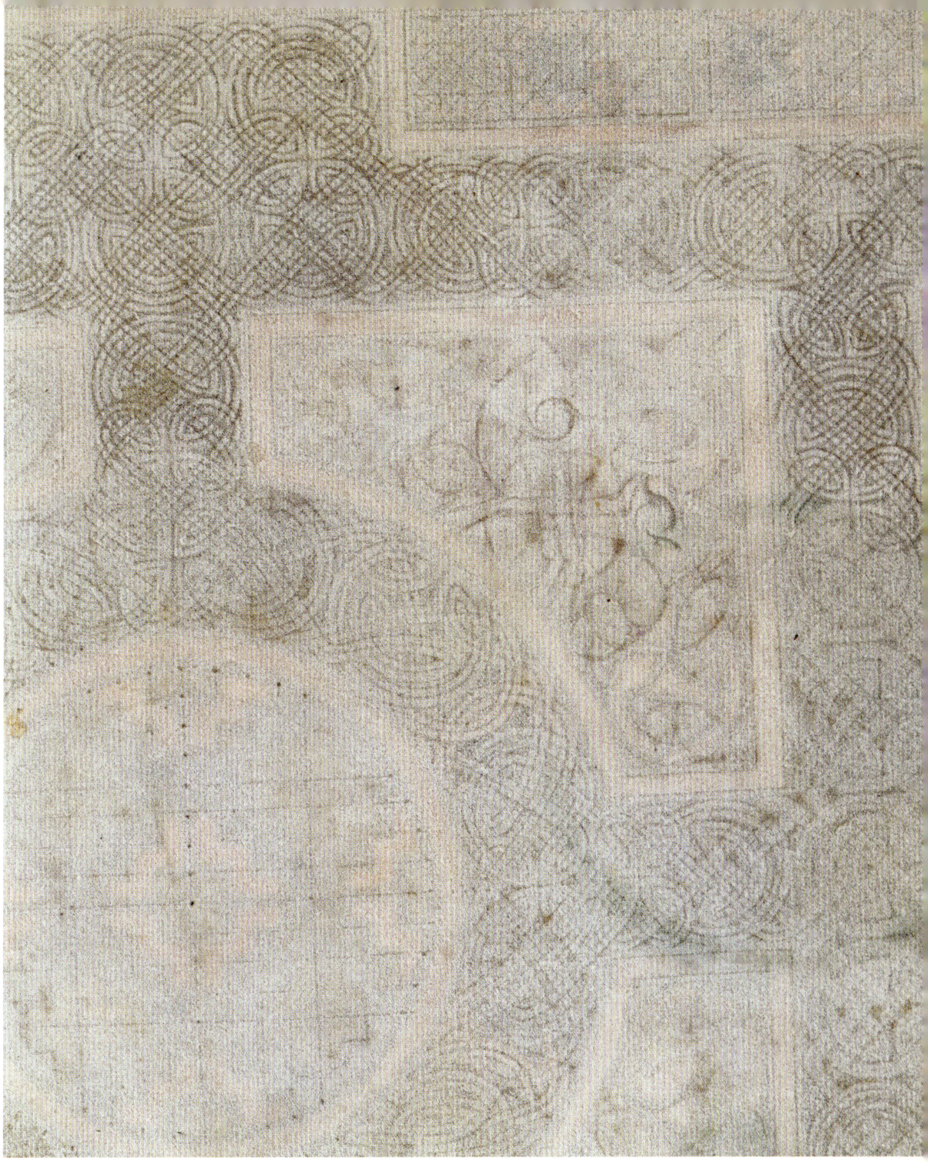

The closest parallels for the art and script of the Lindisfarne Gospels occur at Lindisfarne and areas under its influence, such as the Lothians. Cuthbert's coffin was made there and carries figures resembling those in the Lindisfarne Gospels. Cuthbert's pectoral cross uses the same geometric layout as one of the 'carpet' pages. Name-stones marking the graves of those buried around the early monastery carry similar crosses and the same angular display lettering and 'half-uncial' script that is used in the Lindisfarne Gospels. Sculptures with animal interlace (laid out on similar principles) have also been found there and at Abercorn and Aberlady, both under Lindisfarne's authority.

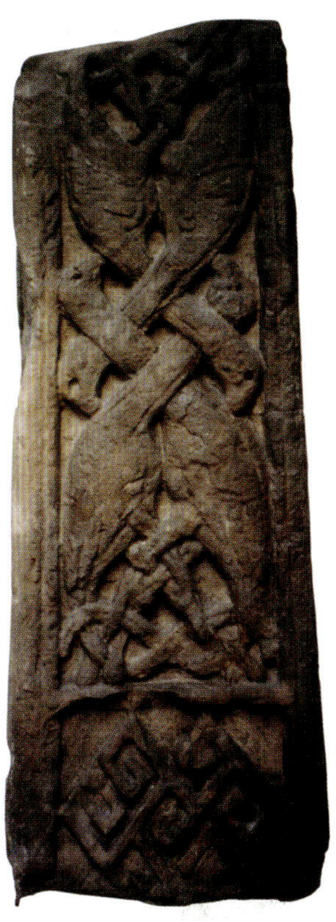

Opposite **Name-stones used to mark graves within Lindisfarne's monastic precinct, late 7th-8th century. They feature crosses, some with interlace designs, and some have bilingual Old English/Latin inscriptions in runes, Roman capitals and half-uncial scripts. (That commemorating 'Beanna' on the far left has script very like that of the Lindisfarne Gospels.) (Lindisfarne Priory Museum, English Heritage)**

Above **The Lindisfarne Gospels: compass marks, grids and lead-point drawings on the back of the Mark carpet page, showing clear connections with the design methods used in sculpture and metalwork from the region. (The British Library, Cotton MS Nero D.iv, f. 94r)**

Left **The Aberlady cross shaft, with interlaced birds resembling those of the Lindisfarne Gospels, from a daughter house of Lindisfarne's on the southern shore of the Firth of Forth. (Trustees of the National Museums of Scotland)**

Aldred and After

In 793 Lindisfarne was the first victim of Viking raids. The shrine of St Cuthbert was desecrated and many monks were killed. Raids extended throughout Britain and Ireland. In the 840s the community of monks and the many laypeople associated with the monastery, known as 'the people of St Cuthbert', moved temporarily northwards to Norham, carrying with them an early wooden church from the site, now covered in sheets of lead (like a reliquary). In 875 they finally left Lindisfarne as their principal house and went walkabout, carrying Cuthbert's coffin, relics and a stone cross commemorating Bishop Aethilwald, Bishop of Lindisfarne between c.721 and 740. The 12th-century historian Symeon of Durham says they headed for Ireland but were prevented by the 'Book of St Cuthbert' (perhaps the Lindisfarne Gospels) 'jumping' overboard. They found it unharmed in the sands of the Solway Firth; Symeon records that one of the bearers of St Cuthbert's coffin, Hunred, was shown its whereabouts in a vision. The monks then went to St Ninian's foundation of Whithorn on the Galloway coast (with which they had traditionally had relations), before turning south, travelling via their fellow monastery at Carlisle and into County Durham and, for a while, into Yorkshire.

This 'flight', from 875 to 883, in fact represented an astute move to avoid marginalisation and a step closer to the new seat of political power, which had shifted from Bamburgh to Viking-held territory focused upon York. The Lindisfarne community confirmed old allegiances and authority as they went by displaying Cuthbert's relics (a recognised means of asserting legal ownership). Symeon's account was probably intended to compare them to the Israelites and Moses (Cuthbert) seeking the 'promised land' – in their case Durham, where the community eventually settled – with the book's survival of immersion in water symbolising Moses' parting of the Red Sea. They headed straight for Viking territory and staged a political coup, deposing the Viking leader in favour of a Dane they had redeemed from slavery, Guthred. The way was paved for King Alfred of Wessex to open negotiations with the more amenable Guthred and begin reclaiming England from Viking rule. Tradition concerning King Alfred's resistance movement even includes an account of St Cuthbert appearing to him in a vision while he was hiding out in the Athelney marshes in Somerset.

From the late 9th century onwards, the community of St Cuthbert extended its authority in southern Northumbria, as well as the northern parts of the territory and southern Scotland which it had come to administer when the kingship had been based at Bamburgh, near Lindisfarne. In 883 Guthred gave it the Roman fort of Chester-le-Street as its new home.

It was here, around the 950s-960s that a member of the community, Aldred, translated the Lindisfarne Gospels into English, annotating or 'glossing' the Latin text between its lines. He also added a 'colophon' (an inscription added on the final page, relating to the production of the book), associating his work with the names of those thought to have made the book originally. Aldred's glosses, some of which comment on the text as well as translating it, reveal concern with monastic reform and abuses of clerical power, and he may even have been 'planted' by the kings of Wessex and those reforming the Anglo-Saxon Church. Promoting the English language would have helped reunify England. Aldred translated the Lindisfarne Gospels into the Northumbrian dialect to establish his credentials upon entering the community. By 970 he had become Provost of Chester-le-Street and visited Wessex on a diplomatic mission.

The community relocated to the stronghold of Durham in 995. There the cult of St Cuthbert underpinned the power of the prince-bishops in what became known as the Palatinate of Durham, bestowing the additional authority of tradition upon them. The Lindisfarne Gospels were probably medieval Durham's 'Book of the High Altar', chained to it and interleaved with records of gifts and relics, offsets of which have recently been detected on its pages. Other prized books were attached to the shrine and to that at Lindisfarne, which remained a pilgrimage site and dependency of Durham. In 1367 a book of St Cuthbert, which miraculously survived trial by water, was also recorded at Lindisfarne. This may have been the Lindisfarne Gospels, but by way of comparison, St Columba's cult numbered some 300 such volumes which survived drowning.

Durham became an Anglican cathedral at the Dissolution of the Monasteries in 1539. It is usually assumed that the Lindisfarne Gospels were taken to London by King Henry VIII's Commissioners at this time. However, the volume may have remained at Durham until the 1590s (when the Book of the High Altar was mentioned in an account of the

Cathedral known as the 'Rites of Durham'). Subsequent dangers, such as the 'Northern Rebellion', are as likely to have led to its removal to safety as the Dissolution. By 1605 it belonged to Robert Bowyer, Clerk of the Parliaments and Keeper of the Records, who lived in the Tower of London. He was a known book-collector and could have acquired it via any number of routes. (If the book had been seized by Henry VIII's Commissioners it would have entered the Royal Collection.) By 1613 the volume had passed from Bowyer to Sir Robert Cotton, whose superb collection became a foundation stone of the British Museum Library in 1753. This became part of the new British Library in 1973. Cotton's book cases were surmounted by busts of the Roman emperors and ladies, and the Lindisfarne Gospels are Cotton MS Nero D.iv, the fourth book on the fourth shelf under Nero.

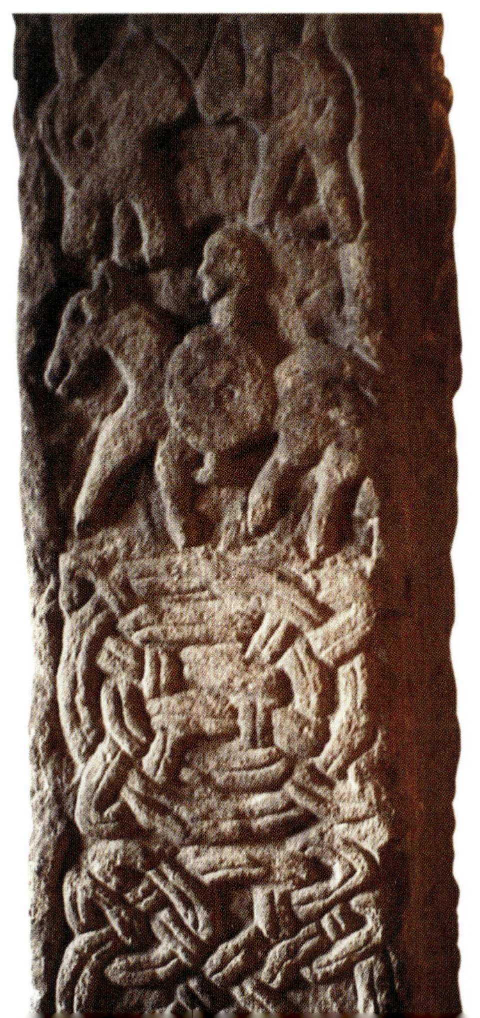

Opposite **Image of the Last Judgement, with rampaging Viking-like warriors, Lindisfarne, 9th century. (Lindisfarne Priory Museum, English Heritage)**

Right **Cross shaft from the 10th century, commemorating Eadmund, now at Anker's House Museum, at Chester-le-Street. King Eadmund of Wessex visited Cuthbert's shrine there in 945, perhaps recorded by this sculpture. Aldred would have seen it. (Photo, the author, with permission of the Vicar and Churchwardens of St Mary and St Cuthbert, Chester-le-Street)**

THE LINDISFARNE GOSPELS AND THE CULT OF ST CUTHBERT

The book known as the 'Lindisfarne Gospels' contains the Gospels of Matthew, Mark, Luke and John, recounting the life and teachings of Jesus Christ. It opens with prefaces and Canon Tables. Each Gospel is introduced by some preliminary matter and opens with an evangelist portrait, a decorative 'carpet page' and an 'incipit' page ornamenting its opening words.

Around 950-60 it was translated into Old English, in the form of a word-by-word continuous gloss between the lines, by Aldred at Chester-le-Street. This is the oldest surviving translation of the Gospels into the English language. Aldred's

colophon associated his work with those thought to have made the original manuscript: the artist-scribe, Eadfrith, Bishop of Lindisfarne (698-721); the binder, Bishop Aethilwald of Lindisfarne (c.721-740); the metalworker who adorned the binding or book-shrine (now replaced by a 19th-century treasure binding), Billfrith the anchorite, or hermit (who died sometime before 840). Aldred says that the work was undertaken for God and St Cuthbert. An inscription added some 250 years later cannot be taken at face value, and Ireland, Echternach in Luxembourg and Jarrow have also been proposed as possible places of production of the Lindisfarne Gospels. However, historical and stylistic evidence indicate that the colophon may be right.

Bishop Cuthbert of Lindisfarne (634-687) lived the Gospel message, travelling to wild areas preaching hope and bringing humanitarian aid. He was a tactful politician, working for reconciliation in conflict and reminding dangerous rulers of their moral obligations. He was a hermit who lived a life of intense physical hardship and poverty – a powerful symbol of non-violent resistance to the injustices of the world and an intermediary between God and humankind. He was the hero who came to symbolise the spirit of cultural assimilation and reconciliation that Bishop Eadfrith and others were promoting in the generation after his death. The Lindisfarne Gospels were a focus for Cuthbert's cult after the community had moved to Chester-le-Street and then to Durham, and the book probably originated with the cult at Lindisfarne.

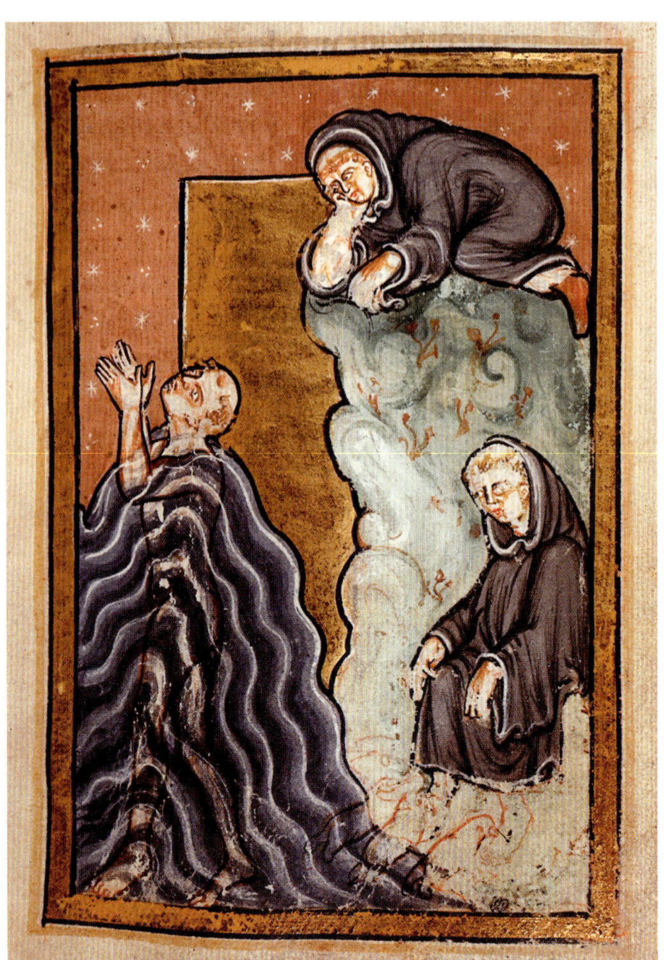

Left **St Cuthbert sleeping, then rising to pray in the cold sea, with his feet subsequently dried by otters, from** *The Life of St Cuthbert*, **Durham, late 12th century. (The British Library, Yates Thompson MS 26, f. 24r)**

Opposite **The Lindisfarne Gospels: the end of the book, with the colophon added by Aldred in the 950s or 960s, recording his name and those whom the community believed had made or embellished the book. (The British Library, Cotton MS Nero D.iv, f. 259r)**

DICIT EI IHS SIC EUM
VOLO MANERE DONEC
VENIAM QUID AD TE
TU ME SEQUERE
EXIUIT ERGO SERMO ISTE
IN FRATRES QUIA
DISCIPULUS ILLE·
NON MORITUR·
ET NON DIXIT EI IHS
NON MORITUR·
SED SIC EUM VOLO MANE
DONEC UENIO
QUID AD TE·
HIC EST DISCIPULUS
QUI TESTIMONIUM
PERHIBET DE HIS
ET SCRIBSIT HAEC
ET SCIMUS QUIA UERUM
EST TESTIMONIUM EIUS
SUNT AUTEM ET ALIA
MULTA QUE FECIT IHS
QUAE SI SCRIBANTUR
PER SINGULA
NEC IPSUM ARBITROR

MUNDUM CAPERE EOS
QUI SCRIBENDI SUNT
LIBNOS · AMEN :~

EXPLICIT LIBER

SECUNDUM

IOHANNEN :

+ Trinus & unus dm̄ euangelium hoc ante
+ Matheus ex ore xp̄i scripsit
+ Marcus ex ore petri scrips
+ Lucas de ore pauli ap̄ti scrips
+ Ioh in prochemio deinde euctuauit
   uerbum do donante xp̄u reo scrips

+ Eadfrið biscop Lindisfearnensis æcclesiæ
   he ðis boc awrat æt frymða gode ⁊ sc̄e
   Cuðberhte ⁊ allum ðæm halgum ða ðe
   in eolonde sint. ⁊ Eðiluald Lindisfearneolondinga
   hit uta giðryde ⁊ gibelde sua he uel cuðæ.
   ⁊ Billfrið se oncræ he gismioðade ða
   gihrino ðætte utan on sint ⁊ hit
   gihrinade mid golde ⁊ mid gimmum æc
   mid sulfre of gylded faconleas feh.
   ⁊ Aldred presbyter indignus ⁊ misserrimus
   mið godes fultumme ⁊ sc̄i Cuðberhtes
   hit ofergloesade on englisc. ⁊ hine gihamadi
   mið ðæm ðrim dælum. Matheus dæl
   gode ⁊ sc̄e Cuðberhti. Marc dæl
   ðæm bisc. ⁊ Lucas dæl ðæm hiorode
   ⁊ æhtona seolfnes mið to inlade.
   ⁊ sc̄i Ioh dæl f hine seolfne
   seolfnes mið gode ⁊ sc̄i Cuðberhti. ꝥ ꝥ he
   hæbbe ondfong ðerh godes milsæ on heofnum.
   seel ⁊ sibb on eorðo forðgeong ⁊ giðyngo
   wisdom ⁊ snyttro ðerh sc̄i Cuðberhtes earnunga.
+ Eadfrið. Oediluald. Billfrið. Aldred.
   hoc evange̅ do ⁊ cuðberhto construxerunt
          l' ornauerunt :~

 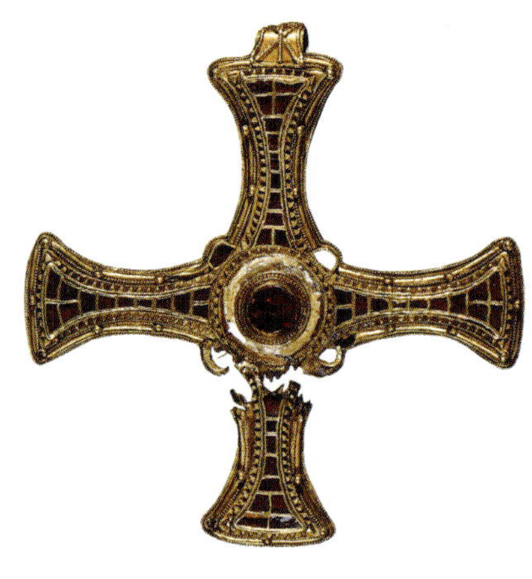 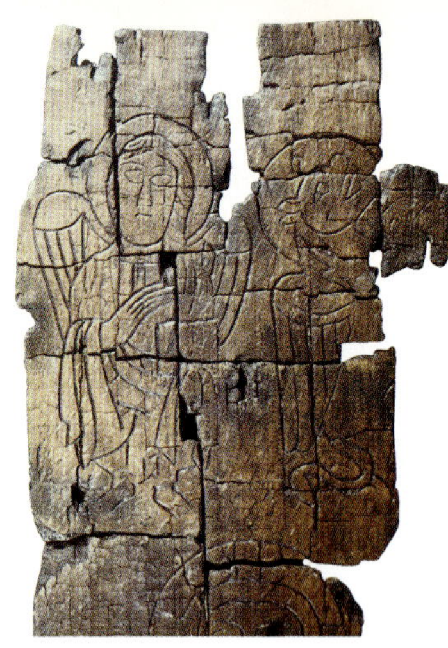

The Making of a Super-hero

Cuthbert came from the Northumbrian middle-classes and entered the Church in his teens. He belonged to the monastery of Melrose (a 'daughter' house of Lindisfarne's, having been founded by the latter's monks) where he studied with the revered master, Boisil. Following the Synod of Whitby (664) he and Abbot Eata moved from Melrose to Lindisfarne to lead the community and heal any ill-feeling between those of the 'Celtic' and 'Roman' styles of churchmanship.

Cuthbert's eloquence, piety, and austerity won him popular renown and the friendship of royalty and common folk alike, both male and female. His advice was frequently sought by the dangerous King Ecgfrith of Northumbria, who saw the benefits of alliance with a potential saint and of using the Church to integrate and govern the territories he seized. Lindisfarne's properties grew, stretching from around York to Abercorn, near Edinburgh. The gifts to his church and the threat of greed worried Cuthbert greatly. He fought this by spending

periods as a hermit on the stark island of Inner Farne, in clear view of the royal palace at Bamburgh – a constant moral reminder (like the beggar Lazarus at the rich man's gate).

In 685 Ecgfrith persuaded Cuthbert to become Bishop of Lindisfarne, a role he performed for two years before dying alone in retreat on Inner Farne. He had expressed a wish to be buried there but succumbed to his brethren's requests that his body should return to Lindisfarne, despite his misgivings that a potential cult might bring too many strangers and the temptations of a less austere lifestyle to the island. In 698 Cuthbert's grave was opened in order to move his remains (or 'relics') closer to the high altar. His body had not decayed – the ultimate proof of holiness.

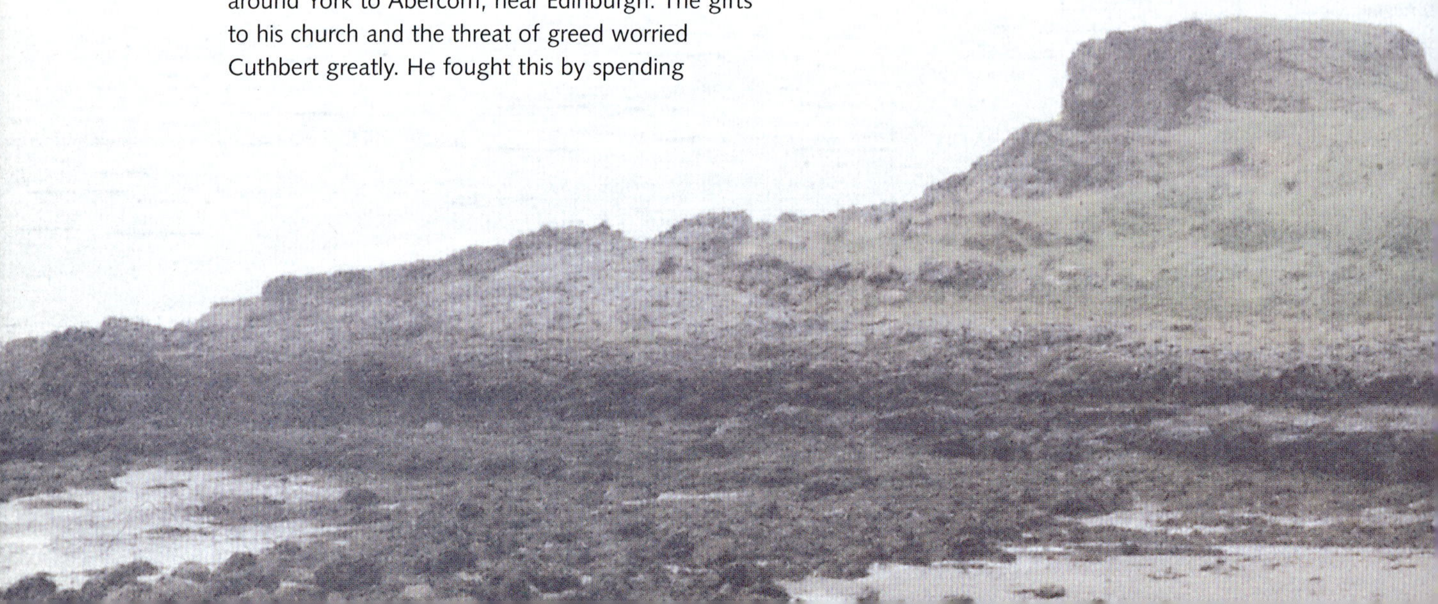

The Relics of St Cuthbert and the Lindisfarne Gospels

Cuthbert's body was housed in a wooden coffin above ground on the floor of the chancel of the main church at Lindisfarne. This was engraved with figures of Christ, the Virgin and Child, and the evangelists and angels, and was probably painted. It survives to this day at Durham Cathedral. In 1104 it was opened as part of the celebrations surrounding the rebuilding of the cathedral and the body was found to be still intact. Disputes surrounding Catholic emancipation during the 19th century perpetuated conflicting claims to ownership of Cuthbert's relics, and a legend circulated that his body had been removed to safety during the Reformation and the secret of its whereabouts entrusted to only three Benedictine monks each generation. When the coffin was opened in 1827 (and again later in the century) to refute this, remains of a body were discovered, along with votive objects placed within over the centuries.

The body was dressed in vestments and exotic Eastern textiles, including embroidered vestments that had been presented as gifts from the kings of Wessex during the 10th century. It was accompanied by Cuthbert's own pectoral cross and liturgical bone comb (made of exotic elephant ivory), an enshrined early wooden travelling altar and a copy of St John's Gospel from Wearmouth/Jarrow. The head of St Oswald, the royal founder of Lindisfarne, had also been deposited in the coffin, as had the bones of Bede for a time.

A major cult would have required a beautiful Gospelbook, to judge from that of St Columba (himself a celebrated scribe) which came to include the Book of Durrow and the Book of Kells. Other saints' cults for which Gospelbooks were produced included that of St Brigid at Kildare (where in the late 12th century Gerald of Wales recorded that there was a Gospelbook so intricate that you would think it 'the work of angels'), and that of St Wilfrid at Ripon. Wilfrid's biography reveals that during the early 8th century, a Gospelbook written in gold on purple pages that had been commissioned by Wilfrid in the 670s (probably abroad as it was praised as a new wonder to these shores), became the focus of attempts to establish his cult at Ripon, perhaps to rival that at Lindisfarne. This may have helped stimulate the making of the Lindisfarne Gospels as a visible focus of the cult of St Cuthbert.

Background picture **St Cuthbert's Isle (Hobthrush), a hermit's retreat in the bay adjacent to Lindisfarne monastery.**

Opposite left **Binding of the Cuthbert Gospel of St John (formerly the Stonyhurst Gospel, BL Loan MS 74), late 7th century. The book was made at Wearmouth/Jarrow and was found in the coffin of St Cuthbert in 1104. It retains its original binding, the earliest to survive in the West, bound in 'Coptic' (Christian Egyptian) fashion. (The Society of Jesus)**

Opposite centre **St Cuthbert's pectoral cross, made of gold, garnets and shell, discovered in his coffin. Anglo-Saxon, second half of 7th century. (Dean and Chapter of Durham Cathedral)**

Opposite right **The coffin of St Cuthbert, Lindisfarne, 698, a detail of its evangelist symbols. (Durham Cathedral Treasury, the Dean and Chapter of Durham Cathedral)**

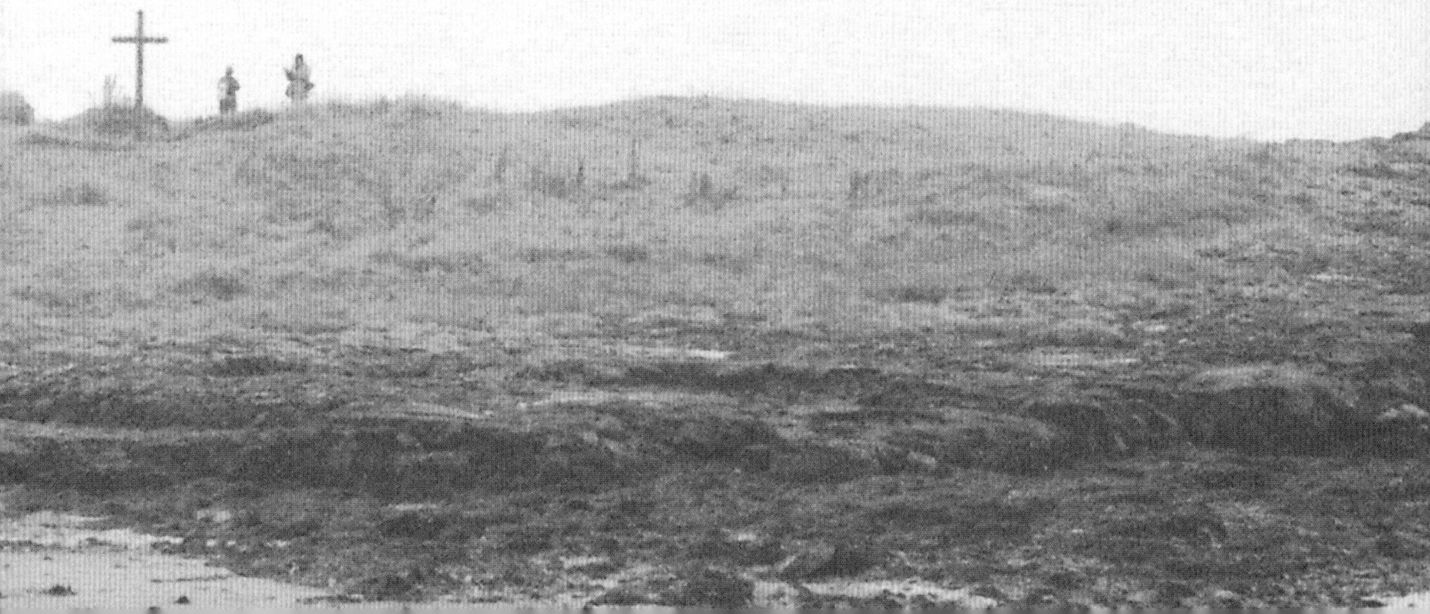

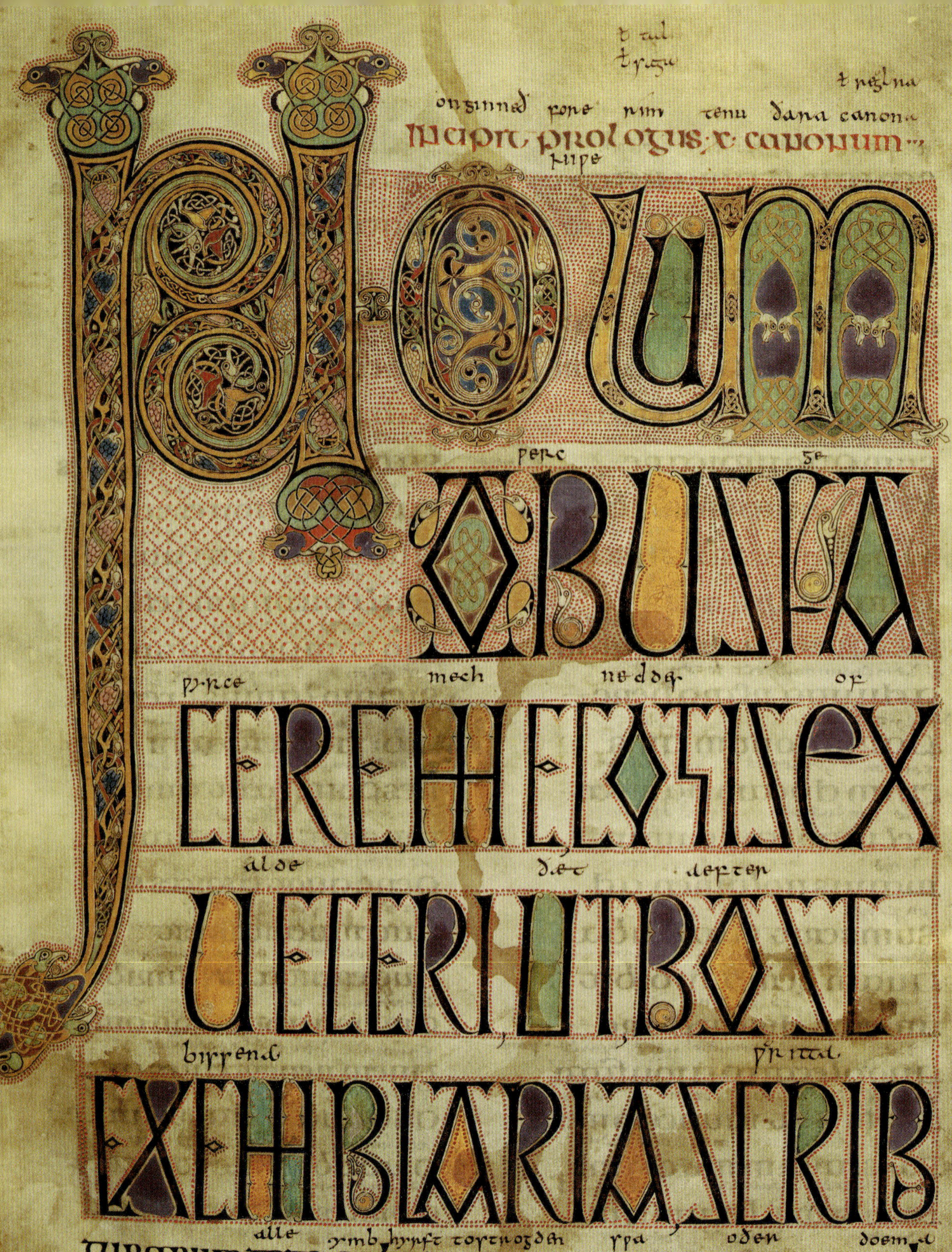
INCIPIT PROLOGUS X CANONUM
NOVUM
OPUSFA
CEREMECOGISEX
VETERIBUT
EXEHBLARIASCRIB
turarum toto orbe dispersa quasi quidam arbi

THE CONTENTS OF THE LINDISFARNE GOSPELS

The Text and Script

The Gospels form the core of Christian belief, along with the Judaic Old Testament and other texts relating to the foundation of the early Church. These circulated in Greek, Hebrew and Aramaic, often orally, but were gradually codified to form the Christian Bible. Under Rome it was translated into everyday Latin, and circulated in many forms. To minimise the variations a new 'Vulgate' ('common') translation was made by St Jerome (died c.420). Aldred's translation of the gospels added English to the 'sacred languages' of Hebrew, Greek and Latin, a process begun by Bede who was translating John's Gospel on his deathbed.

The Lindisfarne Gospels celebrate Jerome's Vulgate version, preceded by his prefaces and by Canon Tables. Each Gospel is introduced by prologues concerning authorship, by chapter summaries and by instructions concerning readings for certain feast days. The saints celebrated include Januarius and Stephen, indicating Naples (which had churches dedicated to them) as the source of the textual model for the Lindisfarne Gospels. This model (or 'exemplar') was also copied at the twin Northumbrian monasteries of Wearmouth/Jarrow and probably came from them to Lindisfarne on inter-library loan. The textual model subsequently circulated in Northumbria and Mercia and other copies were made (BL, Royal MS 1.B.vii, the St Petersburg Gospels and the Gotha Gospels). These others lack Lindisfarne's evangelist miniatures and carpet pages and add different types of Canon Tables, indicating that these features were not present in the Italian model.

The script used in the Lindisfarne Gospels is a formal, time-consuming hand known as half-uncial (developed in the 7th century by Irish and Northumbrian scribes). Its stately rounded appearance was influenced by the Italian model which was written in an even grander script known as uncial. The text is laid out 'per cola et commata', which means that instead of using punctuation marks the length of the line is used to clarify the sense: if a sentence has ended, the rest of the line is left blank. Aldred's Old English translation (the 'gloss') is written in a less formal, tiny pointed Anglo-Saxon minuscule script.

Right **The Lindisfarne Gospels: Jerome, 'Plures Fuisse' Preface (detail), (The British Library, Cotton MS Nero D.iv, f. 5v), and the 'Eusebius-Carpiano' Preface. (The British Library, Cotton MS Nero D.iv, f. 8r)**

Opposite **The Lindisfarne Gospels: the Novum Opus, Jerome's prefatory letter to Pope Damasus concerning his Latin 'Vulgate' translation. (The British Library, Cotton MS Nero D.iv, f. 3r)**

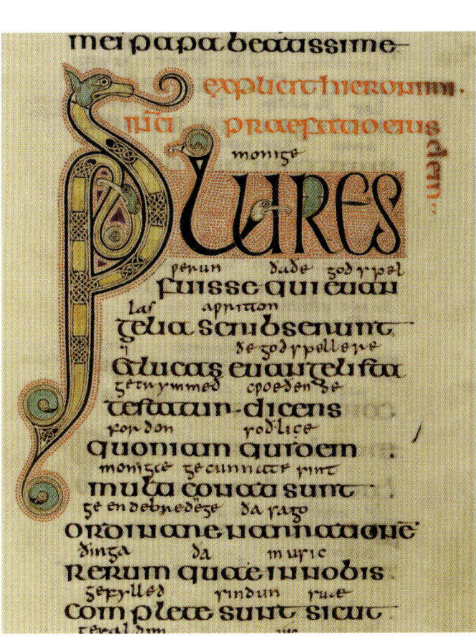

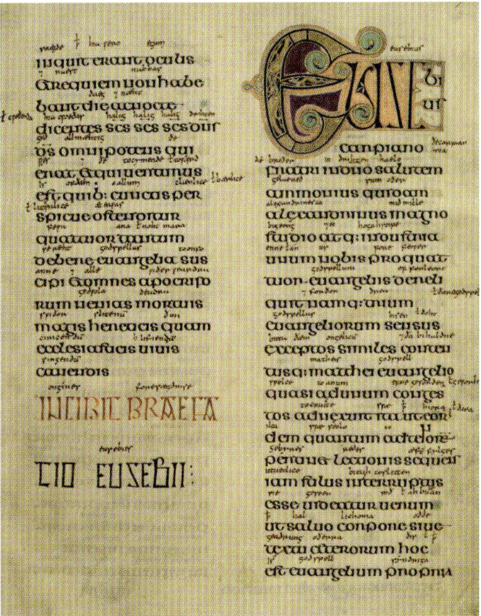

The Jerome Prefaces and the Canon Tables

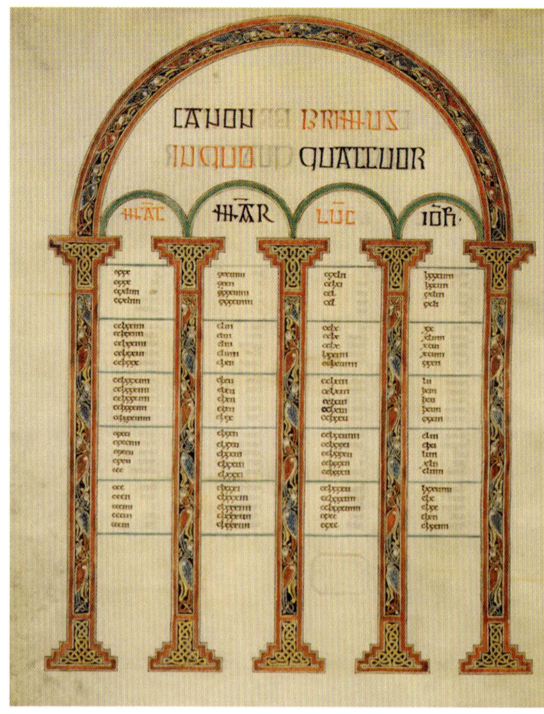

The Lindisfarne Gospels open with a carpet page that introduces St Jerome's prefaces. This one is more old-fashioned in design and colour than the other carpet pages which introduce the individual Gospels, its style recalling the paintings and textiles of Coptic Egypt and Palestine (where St Jerome undertook much of his work). This faces a page of decorated lettering, commencing the 'Novum Opus', a letter from Jerome to Pope Damasus explaining his translation work. This is followed by another letter from Jerome, the 'Plures Fuisse' about the evangelists, and the 'Eusebius-Carpiano' explaining the Canon Tables: these open with elaborate initials.

Then come Canon Tables, a concordance system devised by Eusebius of Caesarea (Emperor Constantine's court bishop) during the 4th century, showing which passages are shared in which Gospels (if a passage occurs in Matthew's Gospel, does it also appear in those of Mark, Luke or John, for example). The numbers correspond to those written in the margins of the book beside the Gospel passages. Some early Syriac, Byzantine and Italian examples are also set beneath architectural arcades. These recall the chancel arch of a church, the Holy of holies. For these numbers symbolise Christ, in numerical form, in the same way as the Gospelbook itself was used to represent him, especially during periods of iconoclasm in which it was considered idolatrous to depict God in human form.

Above left **Canon Table, the Lindisfarne Gospels. (The British Library, Cotton MS Nero D.iv, f. 10v)**

Below left **Canon Table from a Northumbrian Gospelbook, first half of 8th century, the Gospel text of which was based on the same southern Italian model as the Lindisfarne Gospels, but the tables taken from different variant sources. (The British Library, Royal MS 1.B.vii, f. 10v)**

Opposite **The Prefatory cross-carpet page of the Lindisfarne Gospels with unfinished section of interlace above the cross-head. The artist-scribe was not able to complete all his work. (The British Library, Cotton MS Nero D.iv, f. 2v)**

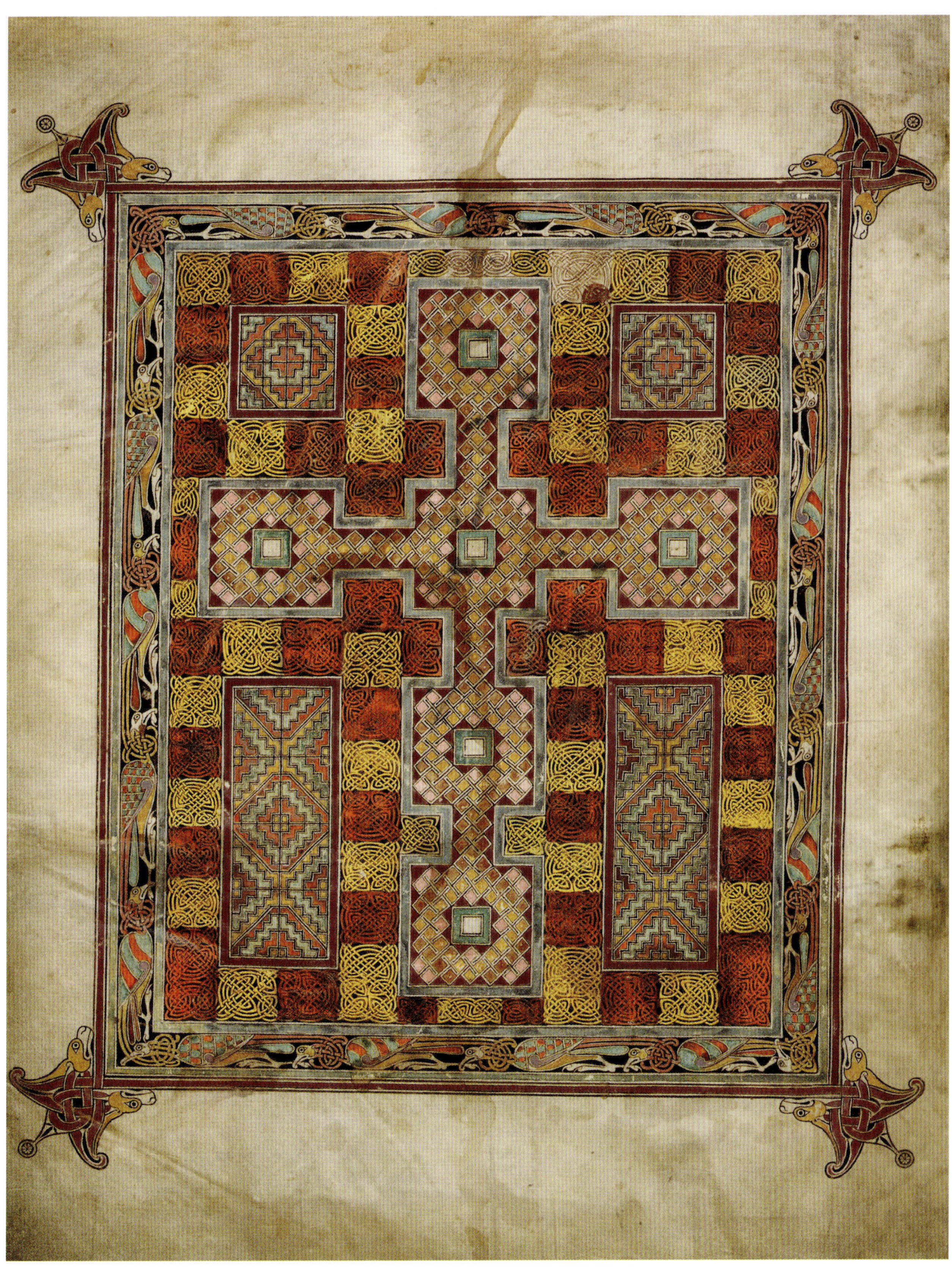

Sacred Calligraphy:
the Decorated Incipit Pages and Initials

Each Gospel opens with decorated script giving its opening words (incipits). The letters explode across the page in a riot of ornament – an innovative masterpiece of sacred calligraphy (an art form later favoured by Islam which prohibited the depiction of the divine in human figural form). The Christmas story relating Christ's birth is also introduced by a great 'Chi-rho' page, the first letters of the name Christ in Greek, themselves a symbol of Christianity.

Roman capitals, occasional Greek characters and angular letters recalling Germanic runes blend together to form a distinctive display script celebrating diverse cultures. The initials are filled with a throng of interlaced birds and beasts partaking of the word of God, and with a vortex of swirling Celtic spiralwork recalling water, air and fire. For centuries Celtic and Germanic peoples had signalled status and power by the metalwork they

wore. These ornaments and symbols were now applied to the ultimate authority of the Word of God – literally the Word made word.

Some of the stylised animal forms may carry distinct meanings, such as the cat of the Luke incipit who has devoured a procession of birds. The cat sometimes symbolised evil, ready to pounce, and was the Celtic equivalent of Cerberus, guardian of the entrance to the underworld.

Large decorated initials mark important text divisions, such as the beginnings of the Gospels and the prefaces. Smaller initials throughout the text mark passages cited in the Canon Tables or readings (lections), read in church services on specific feast days. Some of these feasts were only introduced into the Roman liturgy in 715 and it may be that the Lindisfarne Gospels were designed at this time.

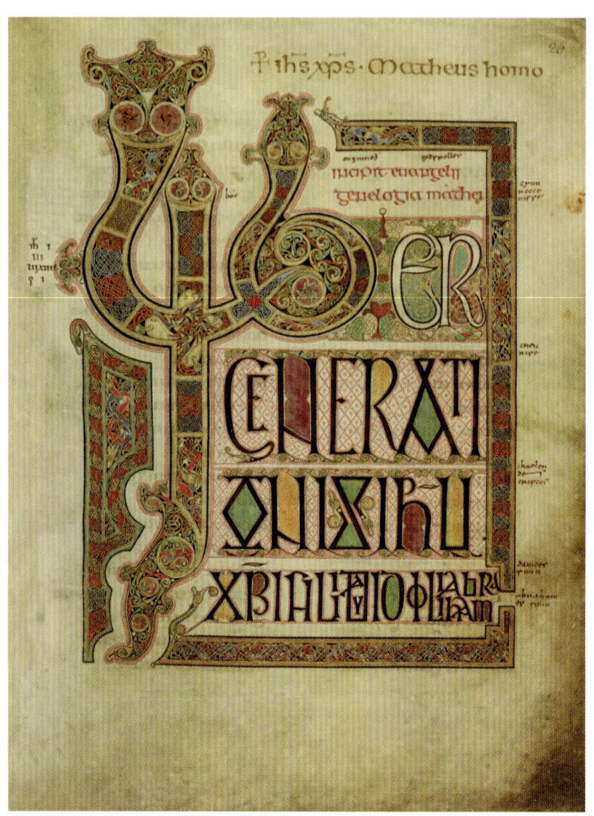

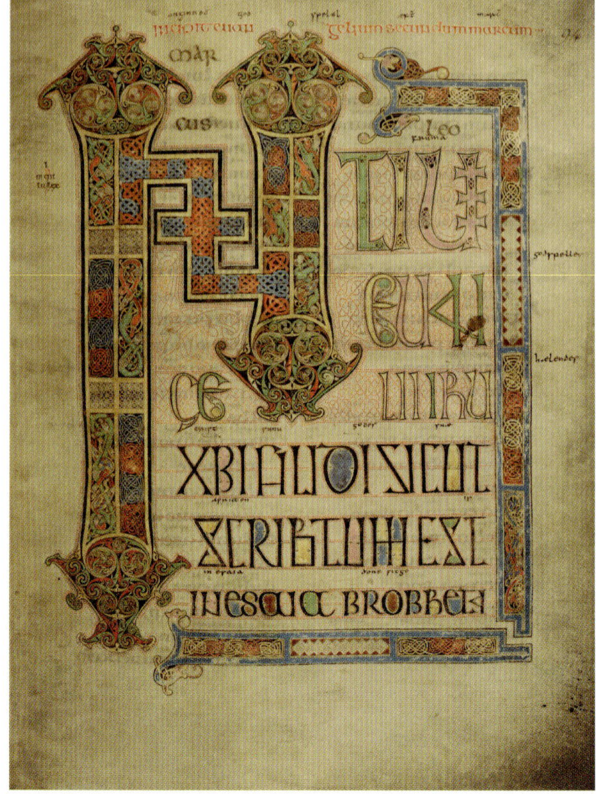

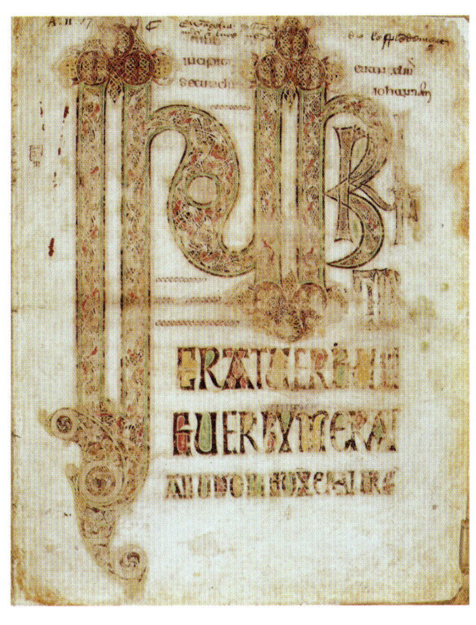

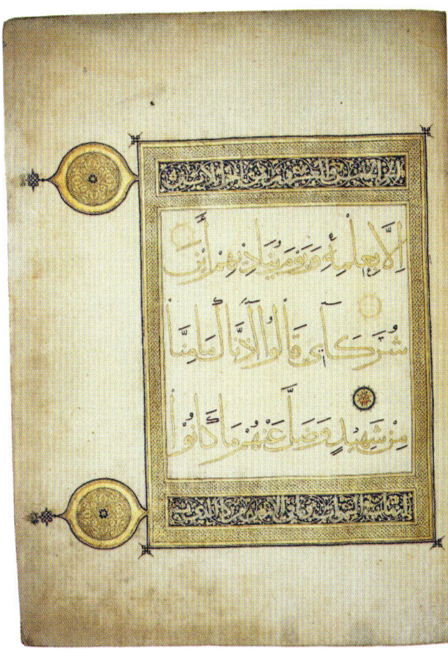

Far left **John incipit page, The Durham Gospels**, probably made in Northumbria and perhaps at Lindisfarne, c.700. (Durham, Cathedral Library, MS A.ii, 17, f. 2r Photo: courtesy of the Dean and Chapter of Durham Cathedral)

Left **Decorated incipit page** from a Qur'an from Mosul, Iraq, 1310. Sacred calligraphy became a prominent feature of Islamic manuscript art. A similar phenomenon is encountered in the Lindisfarne Gospels' incipit pages. (The British Library, APA Or. MS 4945, f. 3r)

Opposite left **Matthew incipit page, the Lindisfarne Gospels.** (The British Library, Cotton MS Nero D.iv, f. 27r)

Opposite right **Mark incipit page, the Lindisfarne Gospels.** (The British Library, Cotton MS Nero D.iv, f. 95r)

Below left **Luke incipit page, the Lindisfarne Gospels.** (The British Library, Cotton MS Nero D.iv, f. 139r)

Below right **John incipit page, the Lindisfarne Gospels.** (The British Library, Cotton MS Nero D.iv, f. 211r)

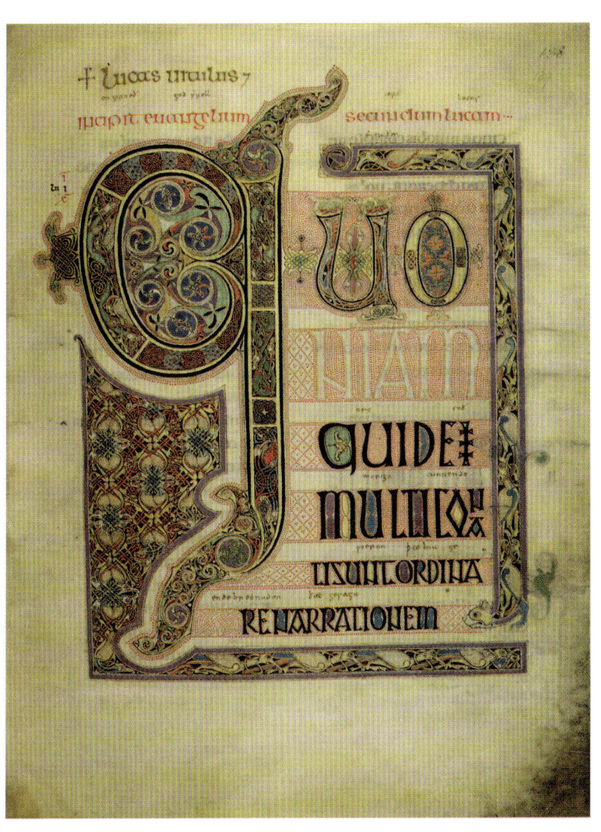

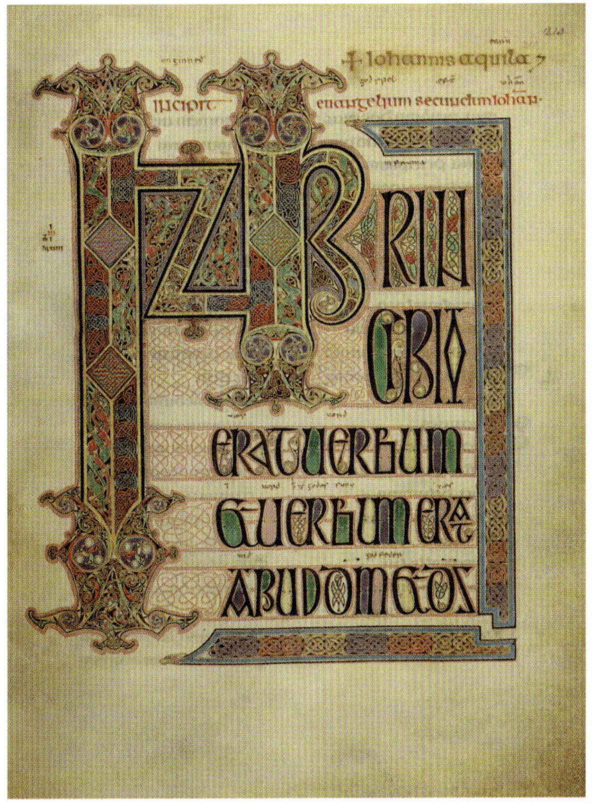

The Carpet Pages

Pages of ornament stand opposite the beginnings of the Gospels. These are known as carpet pages because they resemble oriental rugs. This may have been intentional, for Bede reveals that the prayer mat (*oratorio*) was known in Northumbria, as well as in Eastern Christianity and Islam. Also found in early Coptic (Christian Egyptian) manuscripts from Egypt, they prepare the entry onto holy ground (the Gospel message) and to prayer. They contain crosses, each of different form, stressing the different church traditions and their ecumenical relationship. They also recall contemporary metalwork, symbolising the Crux Gemmata, the jewelled cross which in early Christian art represented the Christ of the Second Coming. Such pages are found earlier in the Book of Durrow (probably made during the late 7th century) and in the Book of Kells (probably made around 800), both associated with the cult of the Irish St Columba of Iona (where they may both have been made). The Lichfield Gospels, probably made in Northumbria in the generation after the Lindisfarne Gospels, preserves a splendid cross-carpet page with interlaced birds, which may have been modelled on those of the Lindisfarne Gospels.

Below **Luke carpet page and incipit page, the Lichfield Gospels, Northumbria?, mid-8th century. (Dean and Chapter of Lichfield Cathedral, MS s.n., pp. 220-221)**

Opposite above left **Mark cross-carpet page, the Lindisfarne Gospels. (The British Library, Cotton MS Nero D.iv, f. 94v)**

Opposite below left **Matthew cross-carpet page, the Lindisfarne Gospels. (The British Library, Cotton MS Nero D.iv, f. 26v)**

Opposite above right **Luke cross-carpet page, the Lindisfarne Gospels. (The British Library, Cotton MS Nero D.iv, f. 138v)**

Opposite below right **John cross-carpet page, the Lindisfarne Gospels. (The British Library, Cotton MS Nero D.iv, f. 210v)**

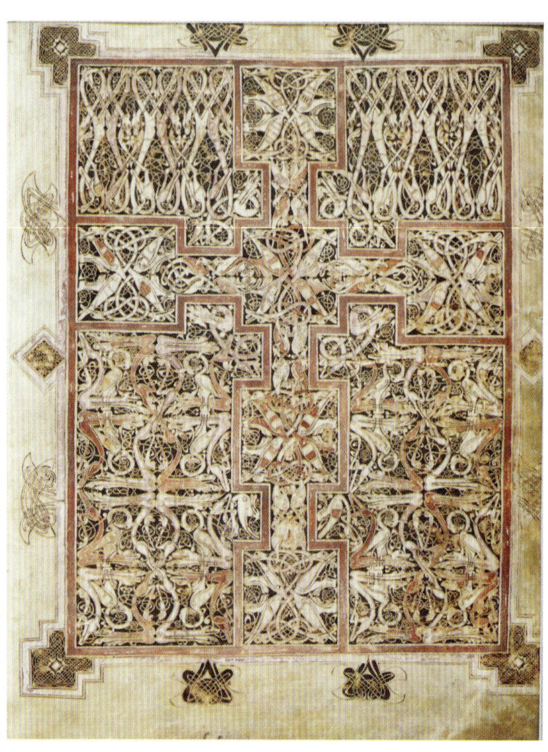

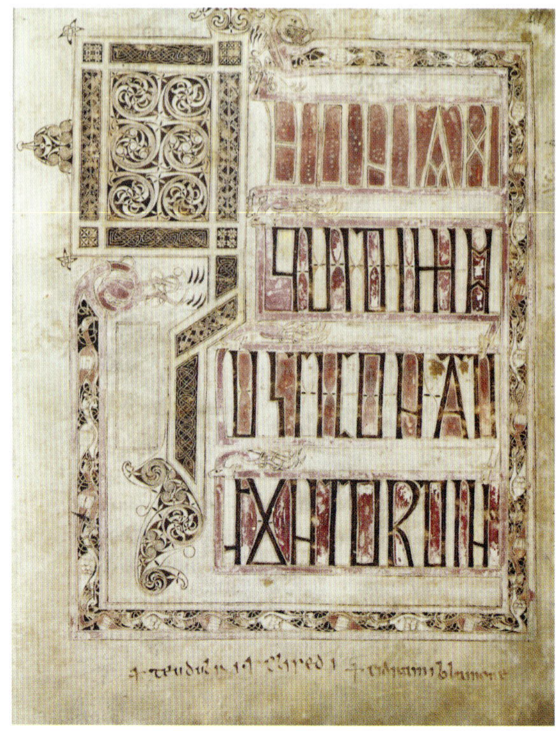

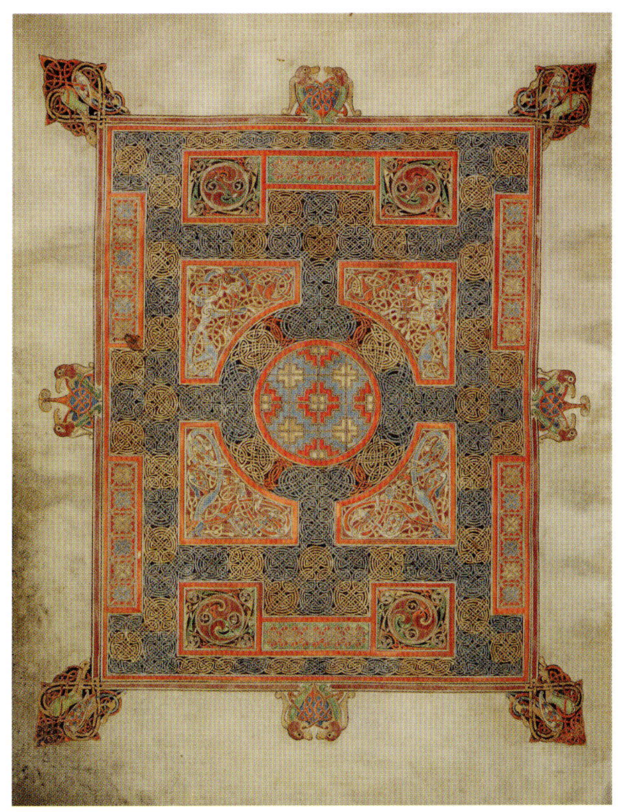

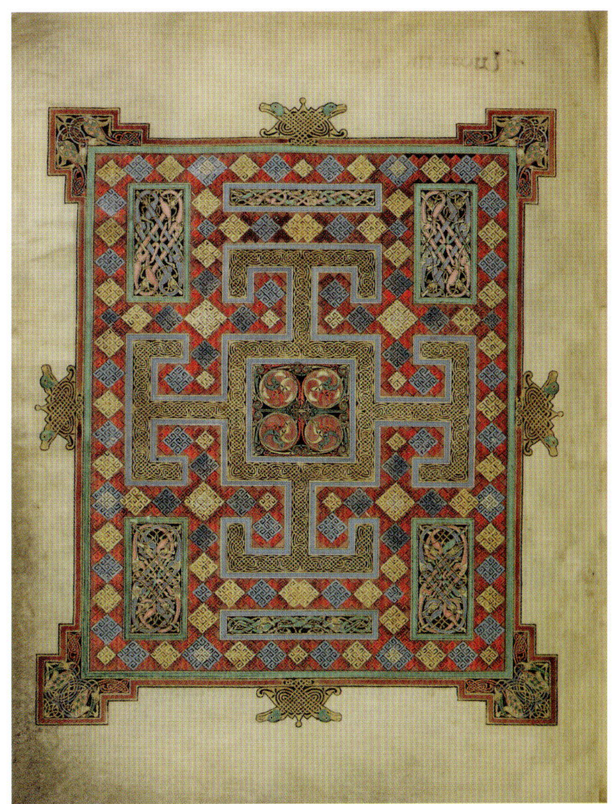

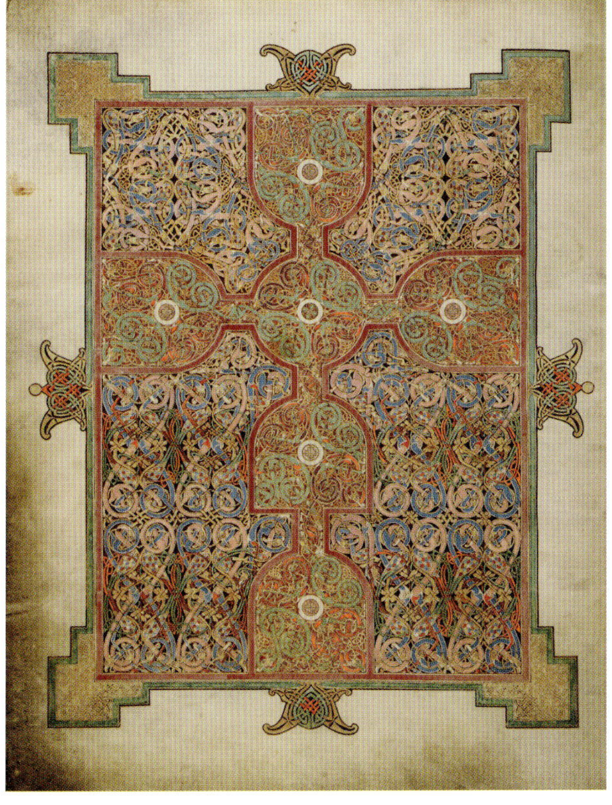

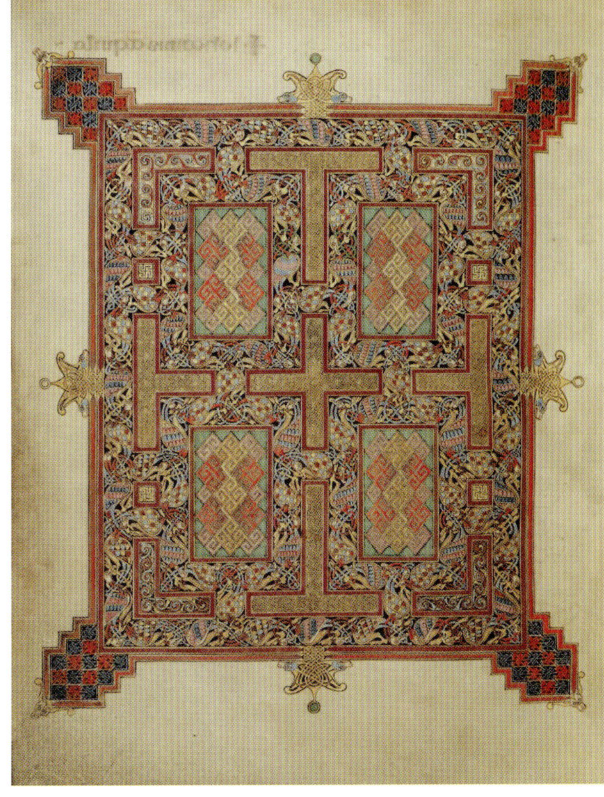

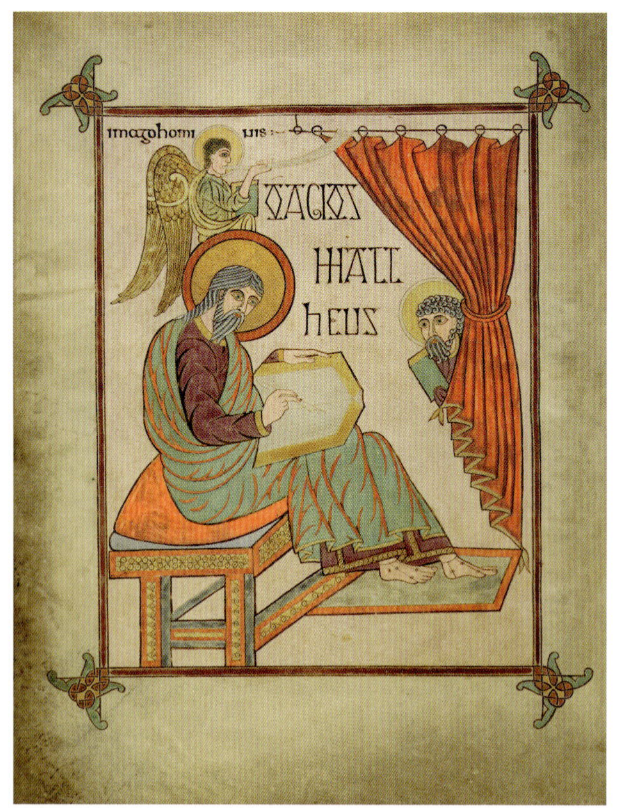
imago homi[n]is
OAGIOS
HATHEUS

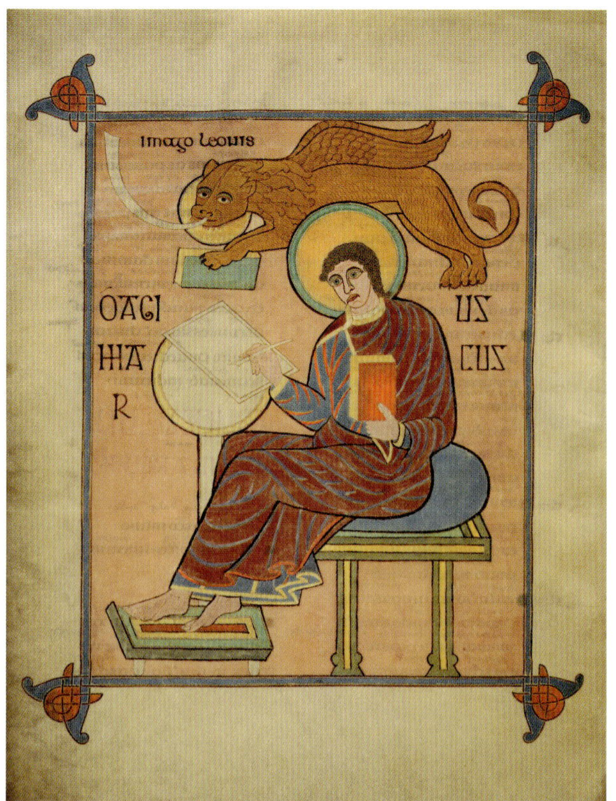
imago leonis
OAGI
HAR
R
US
CUS

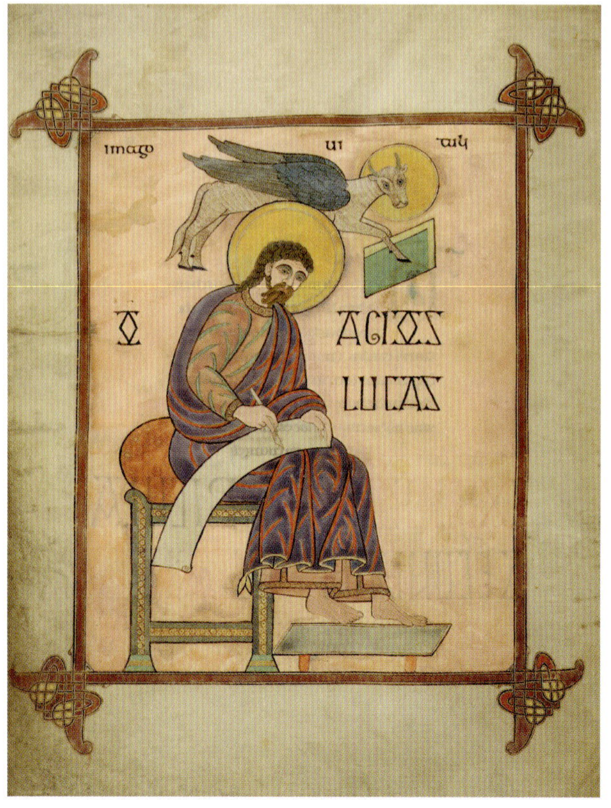
imago uituli
O AGIOS
LUCAS

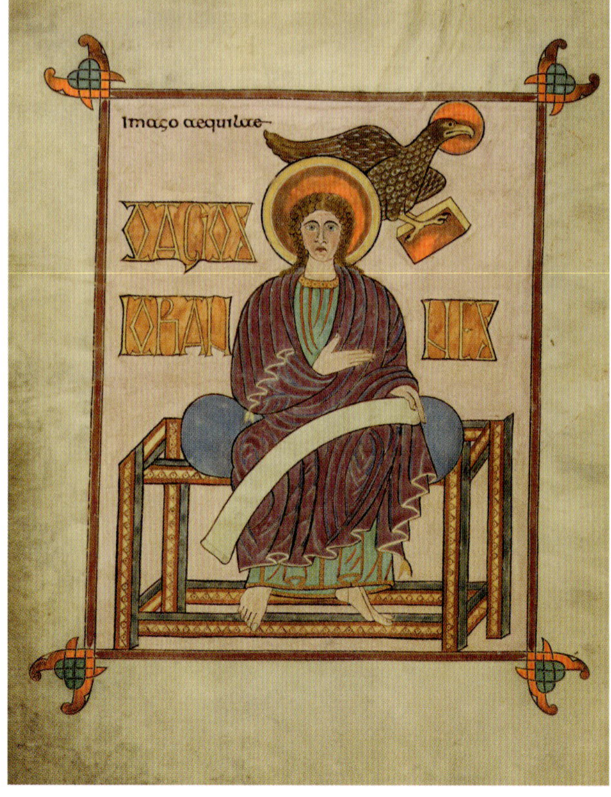
imago aequilae
OAGI
IOhAN
NIS

The Evangelist Miniatures

The evangelists are shown as author-scribes, all writing except John, who sits enthroned holding his scroll and staring challengingly straight at the viewer. He is an icon, meant simultaneously to represent both the Gospel author, St John, and Christ in Majesty, enthroned at the Last Judgement and holding a scroll symbolising the Book of Life in which the names of the blessed are inscribed.

Commentators such as Bede tell how the evangelists were interpreted. Each Gospel had a different character and was represented by a different symbol. Matthew was the man, representing the incarnate, human Christ. Mark was the lion, symbolising kingship and the triumphant Christ of the Resurrection. Luke was the calf, the sacrificial victim of the Crucifixion. John was the eagle, who flew directly to the throne of God for inspiration and symbolised Christ's Second Coming.

The two evangelists symbolising the divine immortal Christ (Mark and John) are youthful and the two representing his mortal nature (Matthew and Luke) are ageing and bearded, in Byzantine fashion. Only two of their evangelist symbols are shown blowing trumpets, as a reminder of the Last Judgement. This is one of many clues that the artist did not just copy a single series of images from one model but composed them himself, drawing upon various sources to make complex symbolic images.

Matthew is joined by a mysterious haloed figure behind a curtain. He may symbolise the inspiration of God or the process of transmission of Scripture – with the Old Testament behind the Temple curtain, revealed by Christ and informing the New Testament. St Matthew is shown writing his account of the life of Christ on earth and he symbolises both Christ's humanity and the role of all scribes who preach with the pen. The contemporary view was: why convey only one meaning instead of many?

Evangelist symbols could also occur alone, as in the Echternach Gospels (probably made shortly earlier than the Lindisfarne Gospels at another monastery founded by followers of St Columba, or at the Insular monastery of Echternach in Luxembourg), and the Cambridge-London Gospels, made in Northumbria shortly after the Lindisfarne Gospels.

Opposite above left **Matthew evangelist miniature, the Lindisfarne Gospels. (The British Library, Cotton MS Nero D.iv, f. 25v)**

Opposite above right **Mark evangelist miniature, the Lindisfarne Gospels. (The British Library, Cotton MS Nero D.iv, f. 93v)**

Opposite below left **Luke evangelist miniature, the Lindisfarne Gospels. (The British Library, Cotton MS Nero D.iv, f. 137v)**

Opposite below right **John evangelist miniature, the Lindisfarne Gospels. (The British Library, Cotton MS Nero D.iv, f. 209v)**

Right **St John evangelist miniature, The Cambridge-London Gospels Northumbria?, second quarter of the 8th century. (Cambridge, Corpus Christi College, MS 197B, f. 1v).**

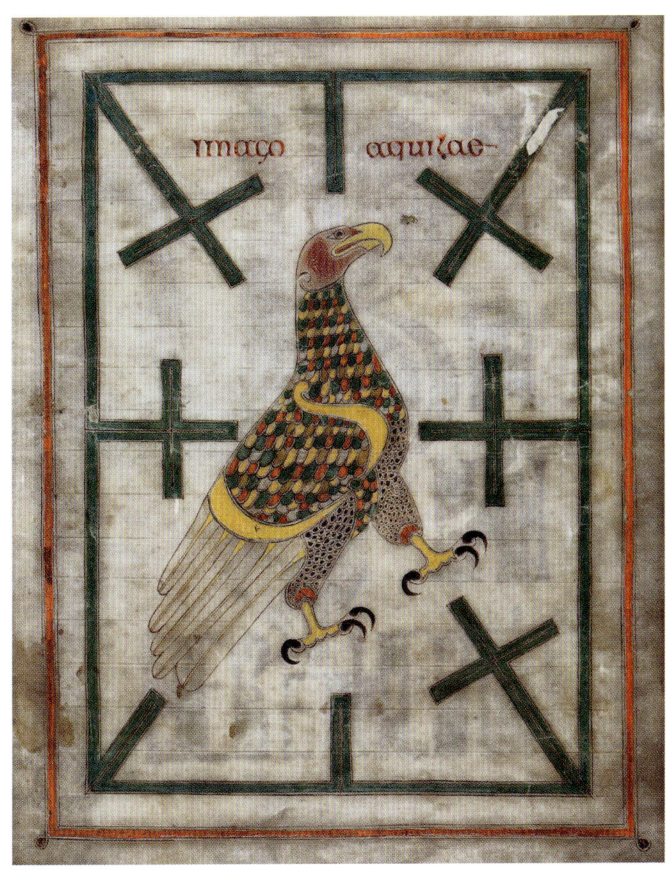

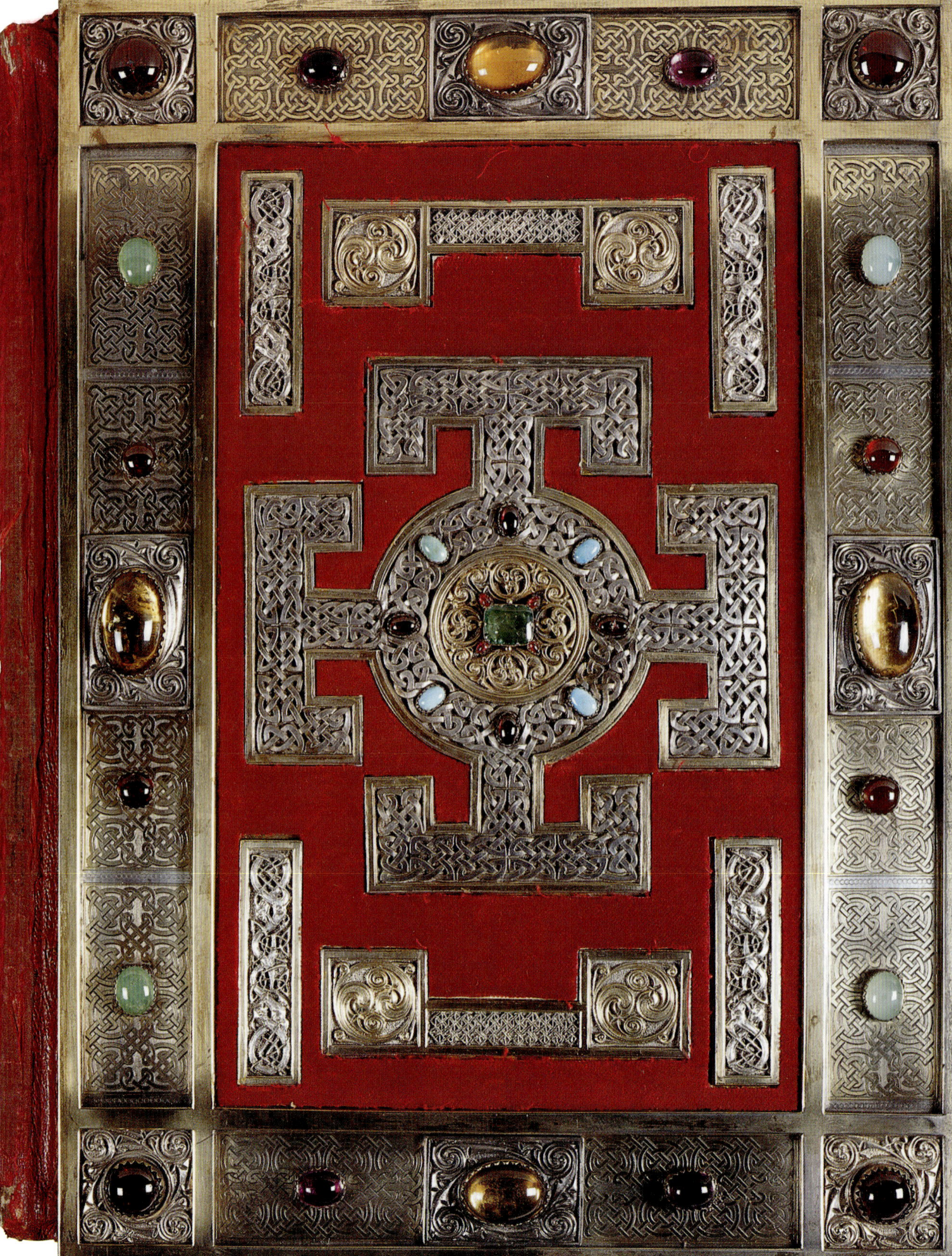

The Book as Icon

Celtic and Germanic peoples possessed rich oral cultures during prehistory. They also developed their own limited script systems (ogam and runes) for short inscriptions, born of early contact with Rome. Christianity is a religion of the Book and conversion brought increasing written literacy. These northern peoples embraced its challenges, bringing their own art and symbolism to book production. Learning Latin as a foreign language, as these peoples had to, meant that grammar and legibility were especially important and Irish scribes in particular made significant contributions, such as introducing word separation and systematic punctuation. This interest extended to their own languages, making Old Irish and Old English the earliest written Western vernaculars.

The artistry of these northern European peoples, developed on metalwork, wood and stone, was now placed at the service of the Word of God. From the 7th century onwards, and especially following the creation of the Lindisfarne Gospels, the impact on books was immense. Decorated words expand to fill the page, becoming images of the divine in their own right. At a time when the fear of idolatry was prevalent in Judaism, Islam and Christianity, sacred calligraphy flourished. However, the West also took its lead from the words of Pope Gregory the Great: 'in images the illiterate read'.

Following the lead of the Eastern Churches and Byzantium, sacred books functioned as relics and icons, performing miracles and acting as communication channels to God. These were books to be seen and were often adorned with treasure bindings or kept in shrines. Billfrith's lost metalwork was probably one such binding or shrine and may have carried an inscription that told Aldred the names of those who made and embellished the Lindisfarne Gospels.

Opposite **The upper cover of the 1853 treasure binding of the Lindisfarne Gospels, commissioned by Bishop Maltby of Durham and based upon the volume's carpet pages. (The British Library, Cotton MS Nero D.iv)**

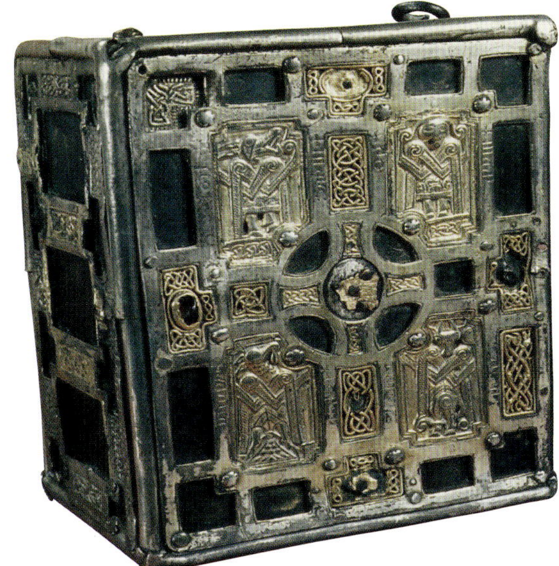

Above (top) **The Soiscél Molaise, an Irish book shrine of the late 8th-9th century, with 11th- and 15th-century refurbishments. The shrine once contained a small 'pocket' Gospelbook. Inscriptions such as those seen here may have adorned Billfrith's metalwork for the Lindisfarne Gospels, preserving his name and those of Eadfrith and Aethilwald. There are fittings for carrying at its head. (National Museum of Ireland, R.4006)**

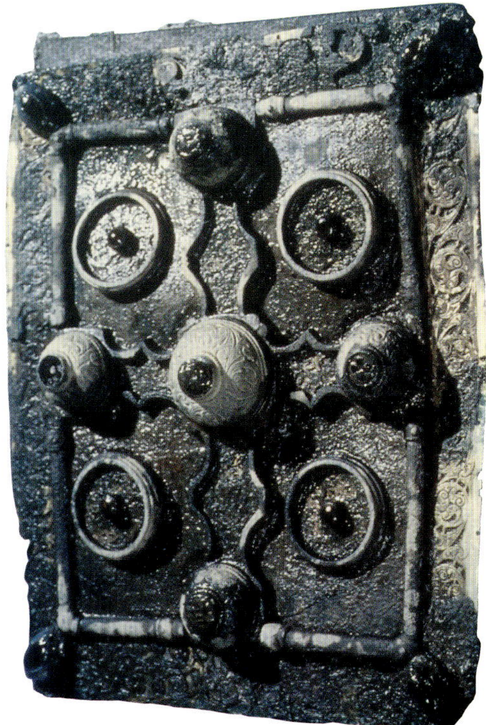

Above **Upper cover of The Lough Kinale book shrine, which once contained a large Gospelbook. Made in Ireland in the late 8th century its decoration resembles Lindisfarne's cross-carpet pages. (National Museum of Ireland)**

THE MAKING OF THE LINDISFARNE GOSPELS

The Lindisfarne Gospels required a lot of planning and resources. Around 130 of the best cattle skins were used and blemished ones were discarded. The vellum sheets were unusually arranged so that the spine ridge of the animal ran across the sheets horizontally at the same point throughout, minimising the effects of 'cockling' (the curling and distortion of the membrane which occurs unless it is kept at the correct constant levels of temperature and humidity) and the resultant flaking of the paint surfaces. This again would have meant that many otherwise choice skins had to be rejected. These costly skins probably came not only from the community's own herds, but also as gifts from religious communities, kings and nobles wishing to participate in this offering to God.

Most remarkable was the commitment required from their maker. Before 1200, and the rise of urban production, most books were made by teams of monks or nuns working in the monastic scriptorium, but surprisingly this masterpiece was made by a single artist-scribe (demonstrated by the intimate relationship between the script and decoration, their consistency and the layout method). This was probably a senior member of the community (there is evidence that other important books were sometimes made by senior people, even the bishop or abbot/abbess), who would also have conceived the project and acquired the materials and models. He was a great artist, calligrapher and technical innovator. His solitary work, like St Cuthbert's role as a hermit, was undertaken as an act of prayer and worship on behalf of all Creation.

Sadly the artist-scribe was unable to complete the final details. Some painting and gilding was unfinished and no-one else completed this intensely personal work. However, display rubrics (titles or headings) and the marginal apparatus (numbers written in the margins to mark chapters and the passages referred to in the Canon Tables), required to make the text usable, were added by a contemporary scribe known as the 'rubricator'. Surely only illness or death could have prevented the original artist-scribe from finishing his labours. Binding the sheets together into a book would have fallen to someone else, again probably an important member of the community, given the project's status.

Aldred's colophon names Bishop Eadfrith of Lindisfarne as the artist-scribe, and his successor, Bishop Aethilwald, as binder. We cannot know for sure if this was so, but it seems possible. The dates at which they were in charge of Lindisfarne fit those suggested by the contents and stylistic relationships of the Lindisfarne Gospels, which were probably planned, made and bound within the period 710-25, with the main work taking place around 715-20. If Eadfrith were the artist-scribe, then his death in 721 might account for the artwork being left incomplete.

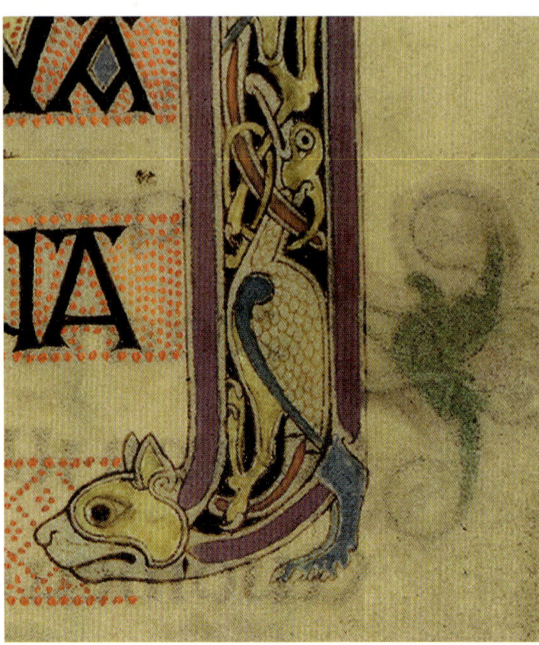

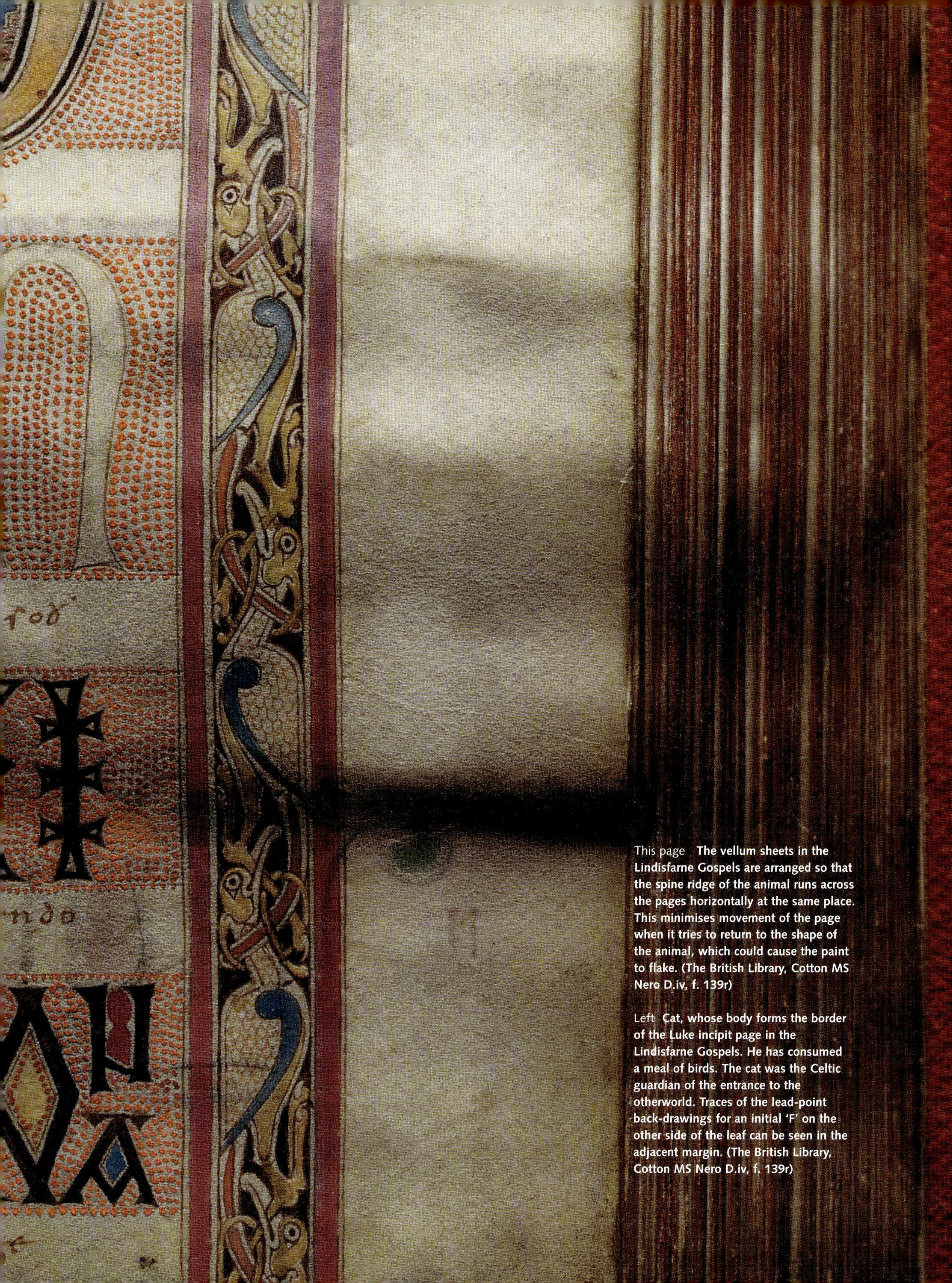

This page The vellum sheets in the Lindisfarne Gospels are arranged so that the spine ridge of the animal runs across the pages horizontally at the same place. This minimises movement of the page when it tries to return to the shape of the animal, which could cause the paint to flake. (The British Library, Cotton MS Nero D.iv, f. 139r)

Left Cat, whose body forms the border of the Luke incipit page in the Lindisfarne Gospels. He has consumed a meal of birds. The cat was the Celtic guardian of the entrance to the otherworld. Traces of the lead-point back-drawings for an initial 'F' on the other side of the leaf can be seen in the adjacent margin. (The British Library, Cotton MS Nero D.iv, f. 139r)

The Art of the Lindisfarne Gospels

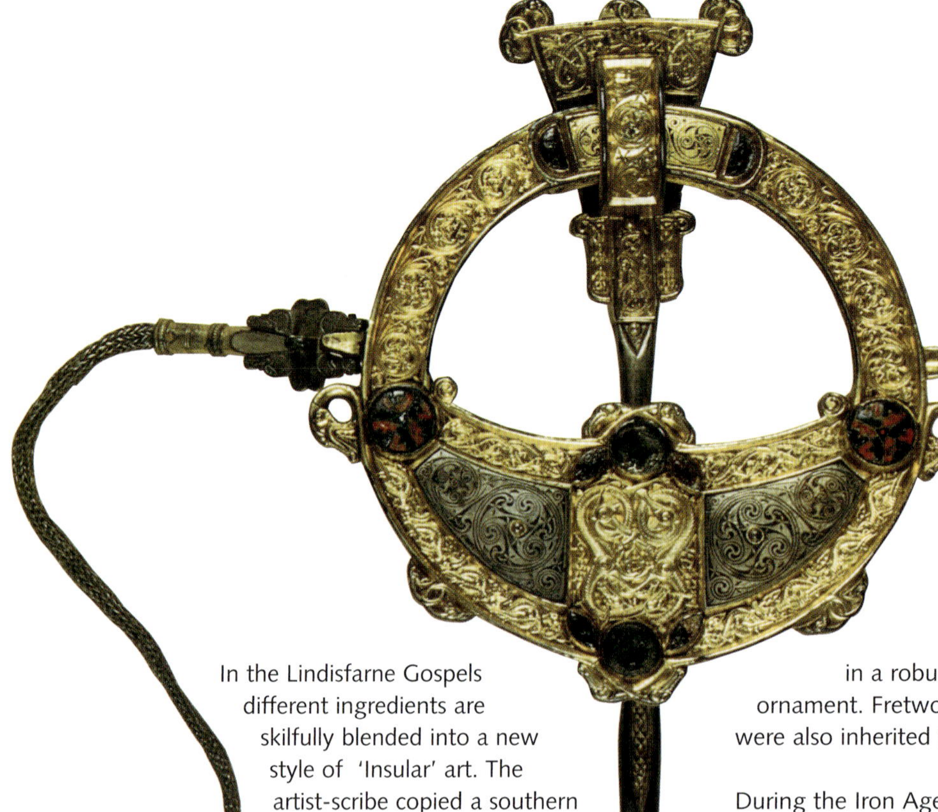

In the Lindisfarne Gospels different ingredients are skilfully blended into a new style of 'Insular' art. The artist-scribe copied a southern Italian Gospelbook for the main text, although he consulted other Mediterranean models for the Canon Tables and components of the evangelist miniatures. However, the ambitious decorative programme was his own and the layout procedure would have been complicated by his choice of a different size of script and by the elaborate initials that he introduced to mark the text breaks.

Interlace or 'knotwork' was known throughout the Roman Empire and can be found from Coptic to north Italian art. Germanic mercenaries adopted it, decorating military gear and weaving in a robust stylised form of animal ornament. Fretwork, step or key patterns were also inherited from Graeco-Roman art.

During the Iron Age the Celts developed a curvaceous, organic style of art, known as La Tène (after an archaeological site in Switzerland). This was abstracted from Greek plant ornament and formed of arcs producing trumpet and pelta (Greek shield) shapes. It also favoured stylised animal and human forms.

Celtic and Germanic art fused from the 6th to 9th centuries and received stimulus from more recent Mediterranean art. The artist-scribe of Lindisfarne mastered the art and introduced his own style of animal ornament, interpreting realistic creatures in decorative fashion. His inspiration came from Mediterranean hunting scenes and vine-scrolls (depictions of plant tendrils and grapes) inhabited by birds and beasts. The latter symbolises Creation sustained by the wine used in church services to represent the blood of Christ's sacrifice at the Crucifixion.

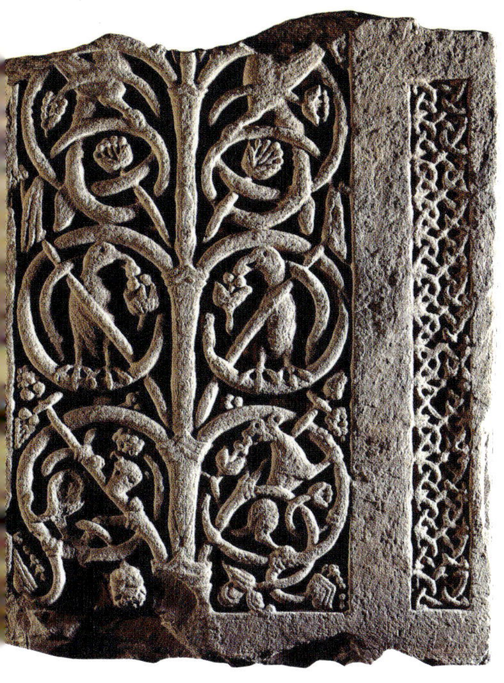

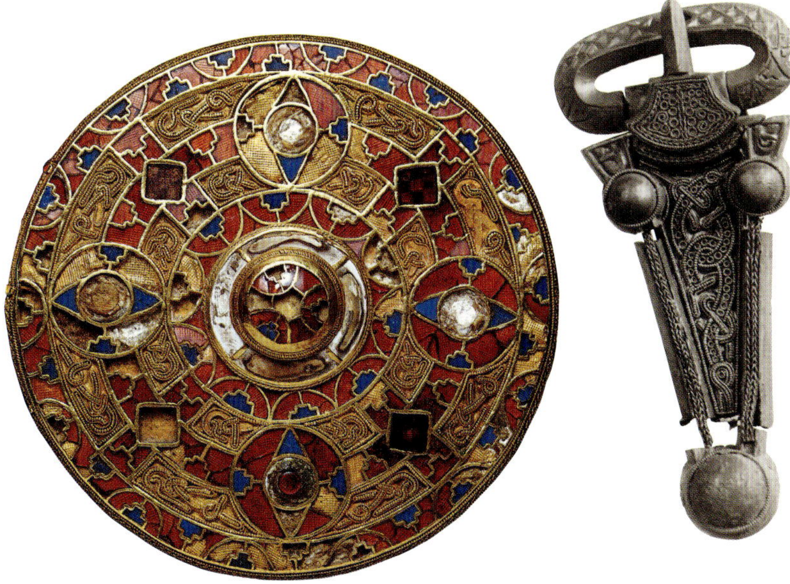

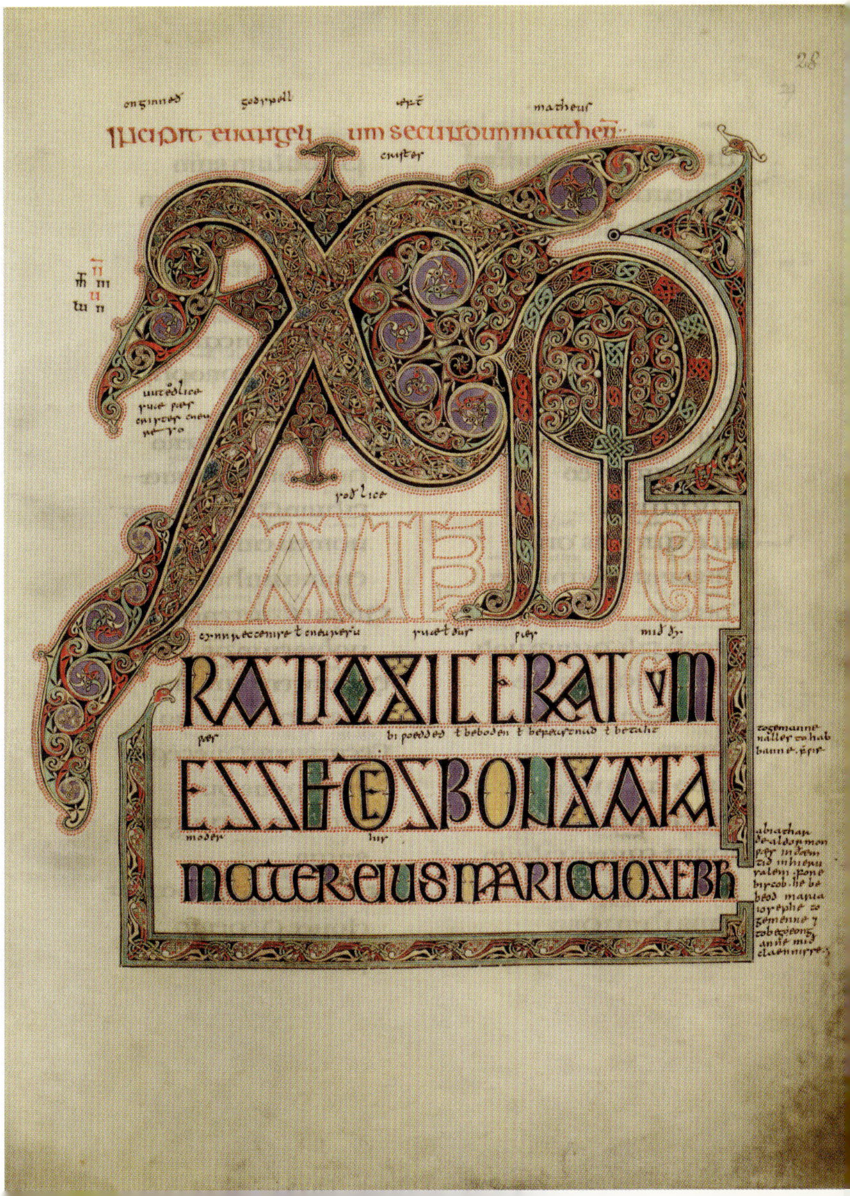

Opposite The back of the 'Tara' or Bettystown Brooch, Irish, 8th century. The spiralwork and animal ornament are very like those of the Lindisfarne Gospels. (National Museum of Ireland, NMI R 4015)

Right The Chi-rho page of the Lindisfarne Gospels. The 'XPI' forms an abbreviation of the word 'Christ' in Greek and was itself a symbol of Christianity. This marks the beginning of the Christmas story of Christ's birth. The various cultural styles can be seen blended together here. (The British Library, Cotton MS Nero D.iv, f. 29r)

Above left Fragment of an altar screen or shrine with inhabited vine-scroll, featuring creatures being fed by the grape vines symbolising Christ's sacrifice. Northumbrian, 8th or 9th century. (Jedburgh Abbey Museum; Crown Copyright, reproduced courtesy of Historic Scotland)

Above centre Kingston Down brooch, Anglo-Saxon, early 7th century. The 'step' patterns recall the centre of the St Mark carpet page in the Lindisfarne Gospels. (National Museums Liverpool, Inv. No. M 6226)

Above right The Faversham buckle, Anglo-Saxon, early 7th century, showing an early form of Germanic animal interlace. (The British Museum, MME 1097'70, Gibbs Collection)

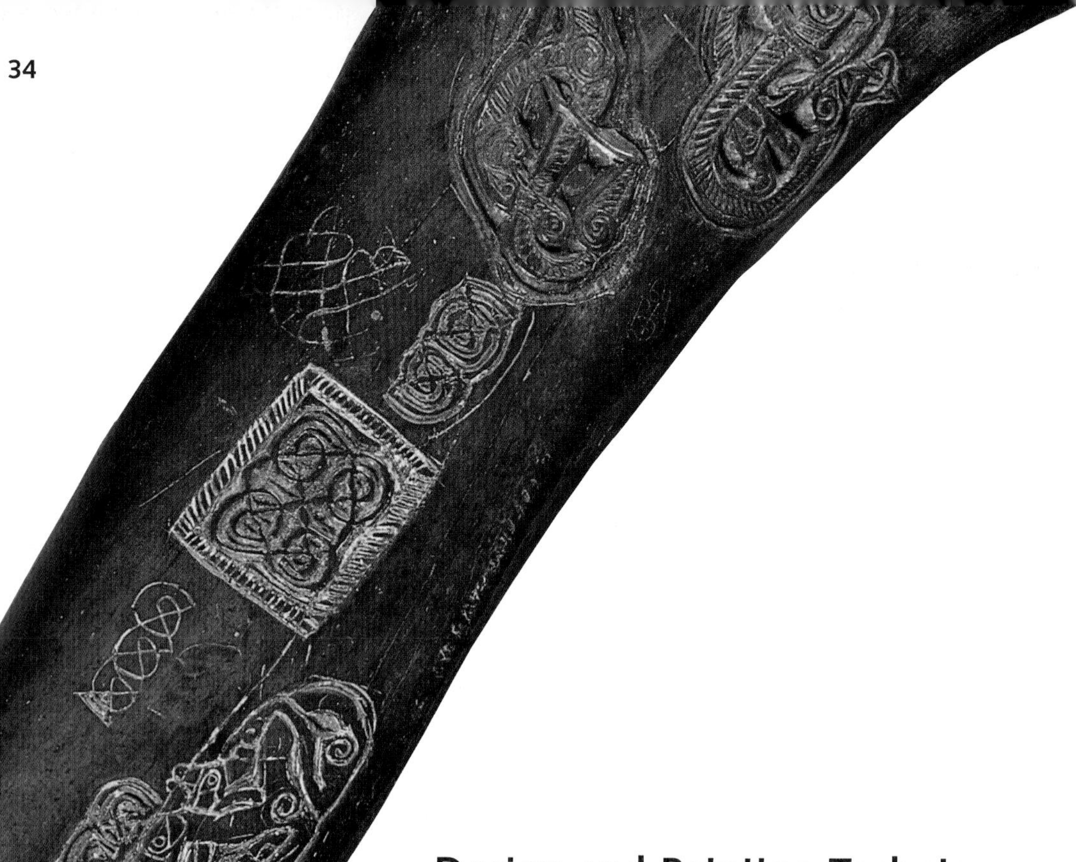

Design and Painting Techniques

Designs were practised on motif-pieces (waste materials) but the innovative artist-scribe used the back of the actual sheets of vellum to plan his designs. Compass and divider marks can still be seen on the backs of the carpet pages, observing the rules of sacred geometry (which Christian authors associated with God's design for Creation). Details were added freehand with a lead-point, the forerunner of the pencil. The use of this was apparently invented by the artist-scribe some 300 years ahead of its time as an alternative to the usual hard-point of bone or metal, which would have trapped the paint of the fine web of ornament in the furrows it produced (as it did not leave a graphic mark on the page but only dented impressions).

Like modern cartoon animators he did not draw on the side of the sheet actually painted, as the first layers would obliterate the detail. Designs on the back of the sheet could still be consulted and viewed from the front by back-lighting, like a modern light-box. This may have been done using a transparent glass or horn writing slope, or vellum mounted on a frame (like embroidery) with a strong light source behind, such as candles, flambards or mirrors reflecting sunlight. He drew the designs in reverse. For decorated lettering, which had to be legible, he may have overcome this difficulty by drawing in lead the right way round on another sheet of vellum and transferring it on to the back of the sheet to be painted by rubbing (this effect can be replicated using paper and pencil). As he worked alone these innovative techniques seem to have exerted only limited immediate influence. There are no early parallels for Lindisfarne's back-drawings, although much later the 15th-century Florentine craftsman Cennino Cennini discussed techniques of back-lighting.

Bone motif piece, waste material on which an artist (probably a metalworker) has tried out his designs, from Lagore Crannog, Irish 8th-early 9th century. (National Museum of Ireland, W.29)

The Pigments

Mediterranean books could feature extensive palettes incorporating mineral, vegetable and animal extracts. Elsewhere in Europe and Coptic Egypt a restricted colour range was used (usually red, green and yellow, which conflicted chemically with one another). Our artist-scribe reconstructed the Mediterranean palette using a handful of local materials and he must have been a skilled chemist. He obtained a range of purples, crimsons and blues by introducing acidity or alkalinity to plant extracts such as woad indigo (blue), lichens and folium (turnsole, yielding purples).

His yellow was orpiment (trisulphide of arsenic). Red/orange was toasted lead. Green was verdigris, made by suspending copper over vinegar, or by a blue/yellow mix (vergaut). White was chalk or crushed shell/eggshell. Black was carbon. Pigments were mixed with adhesive beaten egg white (glair). Ink was made principally from oak galls and iron salts to an extremely good recipe that has not faded. Some fine details and rubrics were of gold leaf and powdered gold ink. These have been verified in the Lindisfarne Gospels using a non-destructive Raman laser technique that involves shining a low-powered laser beam on to an area of the manuscript, causing a few microscopic particles to vibrate. This signal is transmitted to a computer and a spectrum (or 'finger print') is generated in graph form. Its profile (which resembles a temperature chart) is then matched to a database of substances. Such a project is underway at the British Library, in partnership with the Christopher Ingold Chemistry Laboratories of University College London.

Fewer materials were used in the Lindisfarne Gospels than previously thought, making the technical achievement all the more remarkable. There is, sadly, no trace of the fabled ultramarine made from lapis lazuli from the Himalayas, although this was available in England by the early 10th century. By this time contacts with that region do appear to have been established: in the late 9th century King Alfred the Great sent alms to the Church in India founded by St Thomas.

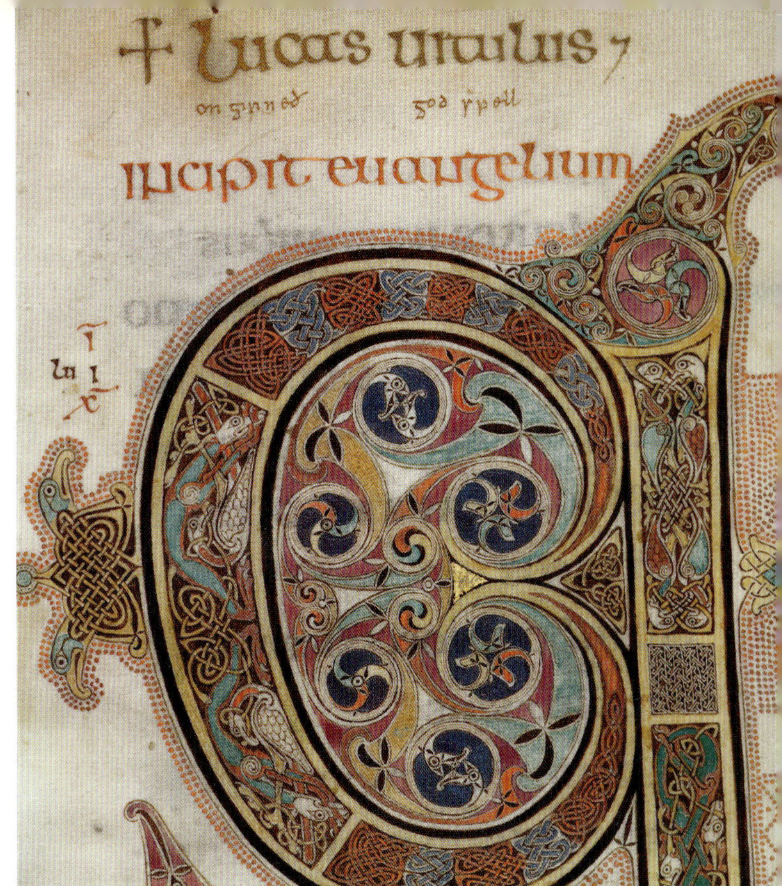

Above (top) **Detail of the painting and gilding at the head of the Luke incipit page of the Lindisfarne Gospels. Gold leaf occurs at the centre of the bow of the 'q' and powdered gold ink has been used to write the symbol of Christ (the cross) and the names of the evangelist ('Luke') and his symbol ('the calf') at the top of the page. (The British Library, Cotton MS Nero D.iv, f. 139r)**

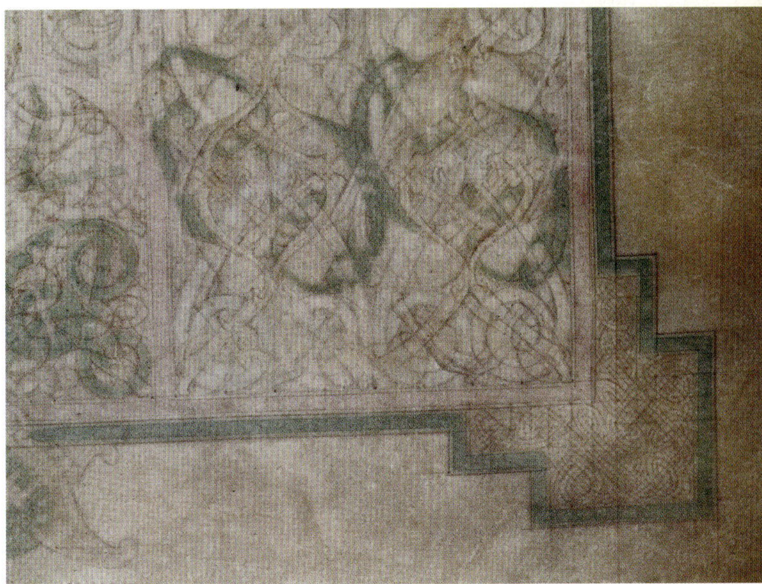

Above **Back-drawings in lead-point for the Matthew carpet page, the Lindisfarne Gospels. (The British Library, Cotton MS Nero D.iv, f. 26r)**

¶ Gergesa. Regio in eos q̄ demonib; uexabant̄. saluator restituit sanitati. hodieq; sup mont[e]
uiculus demonstrat̄. iuxta stagnum tybiadis in quo porci precipitati sunt ǂ

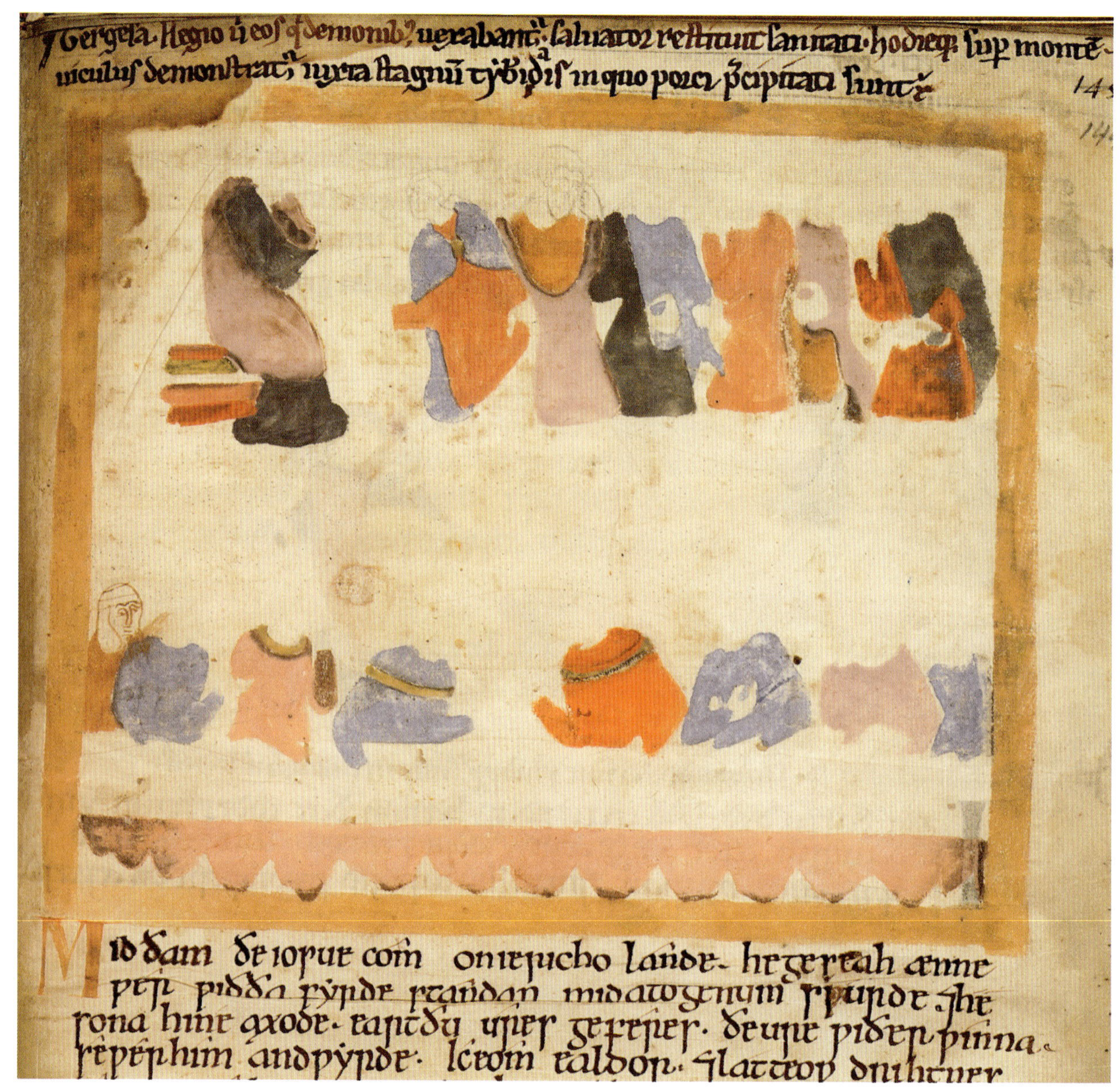

Mid ðam de iopue com oniericho lande. he gereah æmne
pti. piðða rynde rtandan midatogenum rrunde. þe
rona hine axode. eapidu uner geteier. deupe piðer pinna
repeþhim andpynde. icrom ealdon. glattod drihtner

Procedures for Making a Medieval Manuscript

- Soak calf (vellum), sheep or goat (parchment) skins in alum and lime to remove the hair.

- Stretch damp skin on a frame, scrape to required thickness, sometimes adding chalk to whiten.

- Cut skins into sheets forming double pages of the book.

- Prick and rule writing lines with a hard-point (stylus or awl).

- The scribe has to work out how many lines and words to the page, imposing the text like printers would later do, as the sheets are folded into gatherings after writing and the text does not follow on continuously across the double sheet (i.e. if 4 double sheets are folded into a gathering of 8 leaves, the scribe will have to write pages 16 and 1 on the first sheet and pages 2 and 15 on its other side).

- The scribe pins or weights the sheet to a sloping writing board and writes with a quill (feather of goose, swan or crow) recutting the nib with a pen-knife every page or two and dipping it into the ink horn every few lines. The text is copied from another book (the exemplar) or from notes on wax-covered tablets or scraps of vellum.

- Space is left for decoration and guide notes are sometimes left instructing the artist which letters and images to paint. Full-page miniatures are sometimes painted on additional single leaves to allow more time for painting and drying.

- The scribe, or other members of the team, adds the rubrics (headings or instructions), usually in red.

- The artists draw and paint any initials, pictures or other decoration.

- The text is corrected by the scribe or by other members of the team. Corrections are made by scraping out mistakes with a pen-knife (the surface of the membrane is restored by pouncing – dusting powder contained in a small fabric bag), by scoring through, by marking with a point below the line or by adding words between lines or in margins.

- The sheets are folded into gatherings, arranged in sequence and sewn together. The usual Western fashion was to sew them on to leather cords but an Eastern 'Coptic' technique of sewing gatherings to each other, using two needles and thread in a figure-of-eight motion, was also known in early Northumbria.

- The ends of the cords (or the sewing threads in the case of the Coptic technique) are laced through holes drilled into wooden covers and pegged in place with wooden dowels. The boards can then be covered with leather and decorated by tooling or with metalwork, ivories or textiles. Thongs or, later, clasps hold the covers together as skins will attempt to return to the shape of the animal, unless kept at stable levels of temperature and humidity. Such movement can cause the pigments to flake.

Opposite **The Aelfric Hexateuch (a paraphrase of part of the Old Testament in Old English), Canterbury, early 11th century (unfinished). Some of the under-drawings are in lead-point (and this was previously thought to be one of the earliest examples of this medium, which may actually have been 'invented' by the artist-scribe of the Lindisfarne Gospels). The thick pigment layers rapidly obscure the drawings' details. The script is written before the pictures are painted. (The British Library, Cotton MS Claudius B.iv, f. 144r)**

THE WORLD OF THE LINDISFARNE GOSPELS

Travel, Trade and Ideas

What did the Anglo-Saxons know of the world? More people travelled than we might think and water was a highway. They inherited some knowledge of geography and natural history from Rome. Bede's scholarship embraced the natural world as part of his quest to understand God's purpose. Numbers and calculation intrigued him, especially dating. He popularised dating from the birth of Christ: BC (before Christ) and AD ('Anno Domini', the year of the Lord), skilfully converting the many other dating systems he encountered.

Bede knew that the earth was round and wrote of the Temple and Tabernacle in Jerusalem, even producing a plan. In the late 7th century a Frankish bishop named Arculf was blown off-course to Iona on his return from the Holy Land. He dictated his pilgrim guide to Iona's Abbot, Adomnán, and it was rewritten by Bede. Such texts provided a glimpse of a far-off region, to which people could travel, both physically, and spiritually in the mind (Bede never left Northumbria).

Insular missionaries spread Christianity abroad. The Irish saint Columbanus' foundations included Luxeuil in southern France, St Gall in Switzerland and Bobbio in northern Italy. The English saint Willibrord founded Echternach (Luxembourg) and Utrecht as part of an Irish-led, part-Northumbrian mission, and Boniface from Devon worked in Frisia, assisted by his female relative, St Leoba. Boniface wrote to the Archbishop of Canterbury requesting that he prevent so many Englishwomen travelling abroad as many were killed and, he said, there was not a brothel this side of Rome without them.

Trade flourished in some early northern European towns such as London, Southampton and Ipswich. Monasteries and courts also served as distribution centres for imports and manufactured goods. Exotic items from distant parts were greatly prized and brought some knowledge of other cultures.

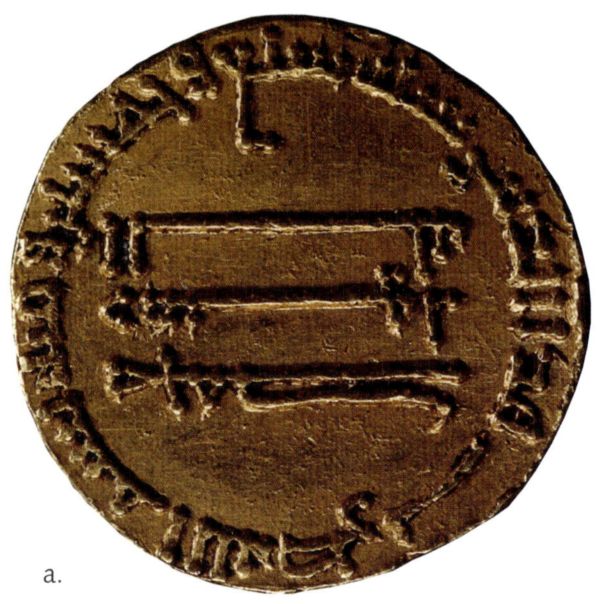

a.

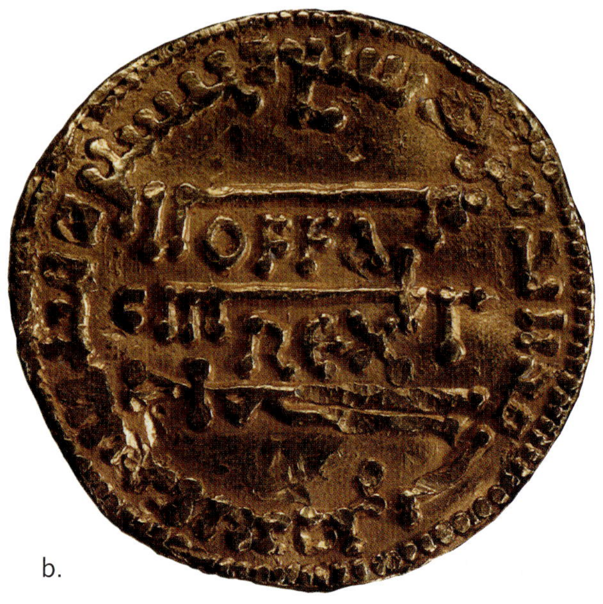

b.

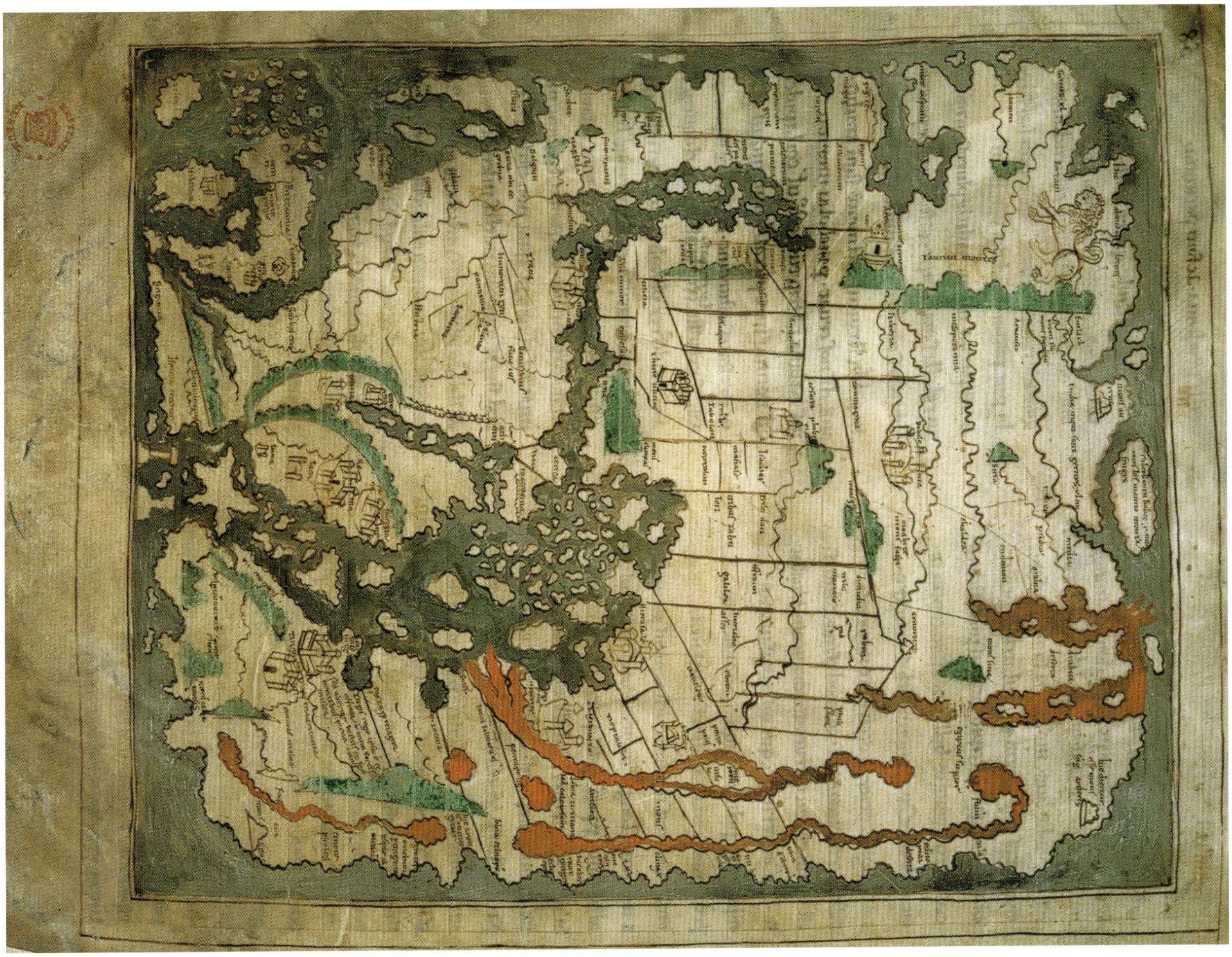

Opposite (a) Dinar of the Abbasid Caliph al-Mansur, AD 773/4 (British Museum, CM, 1860, 12-31-7). (b) Dinar/mancus of King Offa of Mercia, AD 773/4 (British Museum, CM, 1913, 12-13-1). King Offa (whose name is inserted into the centre of the design on the Anglo-Saxon version of the coin) celebrated his role on the world stage by copying an Arabic coin.

Above The Anglo-Saxon world view: a map of the world made at Canterbury in the early 11th century. The image has been rotated to show North at the top, but in the original manuscript Britain is in the lower left and Jerusalem at the centre. (The British Library, Cotton MS Tiberius B.v, f.57r)

Left Portable sundial and calendar, Constantinople?, c.500. (Science Museum 1983-1393). Such devices, or tables in books, helped to calculate dates such as Easter.

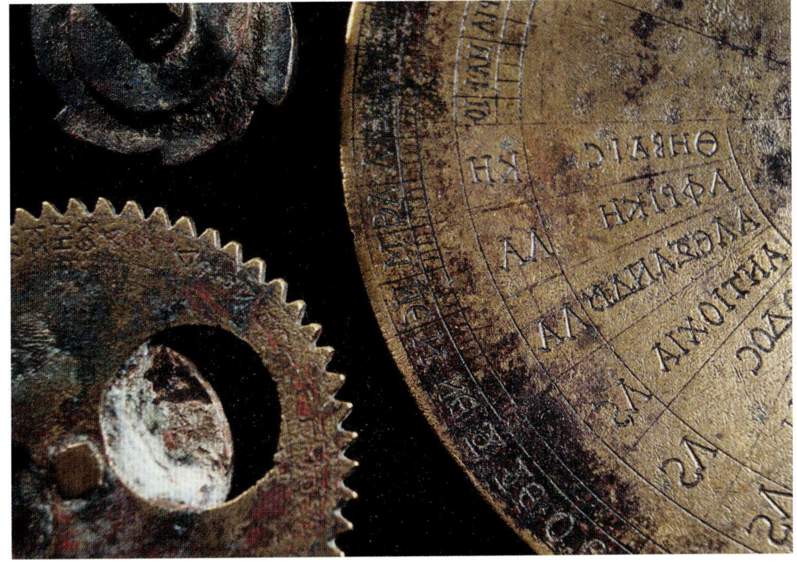

East of Eden: Beyond the 'Known' World

Insular experience of the world may have ended with the Middle East, but the Silk Road linked it, and Byzantium, to great oriental cities such as XiangAn. The islands of Britain and Ireland were linked to those of Japan by an international trade network, even if they did not know of each other's existence. Islamic areas provided a route for Eastern technology to reach the West. In the 8th century paper-making was learned by Islamic peoples from Chinese captives, reaching Europe via Spain and Sicily in the 12th century; likewise silk manufacture. Many aspects of Graeco-Roman learning and medicine were preserved by Islamic scholars and reintroduced to Europe during the 12th and 13th centuries following the Crusades and the establishment of universities.

Graeco-Roman legacies were felt in the farthest points of East and West, but developed in different ways. It is important to compare like with like as many of the scientific and artistic splendours of the Orient and Islam date from later periods than the 8th century. Others are earlier. The Chinese had developed printing from woodblocks as early as the 8th century, while the West had to await the 15th century for moveable type printing.

Buddhism was still being introduced to Japan from China around 600, as Christianity was reintroduced to England from mainland Europe. Echoes of Northumbrian Christian iconography can be seen in Japanese Buddhist images, perhaps reflecting shared points of

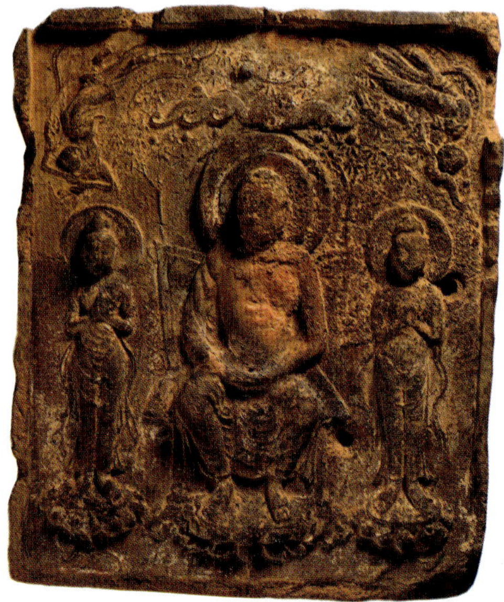

reference somewhere in the distant past. Other arts, such as poetry and music, flourished in both Britain and Japan. Celtic poets were the first in the West to celebrate Nature, while the Anglo-Saxons brought the epic verse of the mead hall to bear upon both secular and religious themes, for example 'Beowulf' (written down around the year 1000) and the 8th-century 'Dream of the Rood'. Some of the finest Japanese poetry likewise survives from this period, notably that by Kakinomoto no Hitomaro.

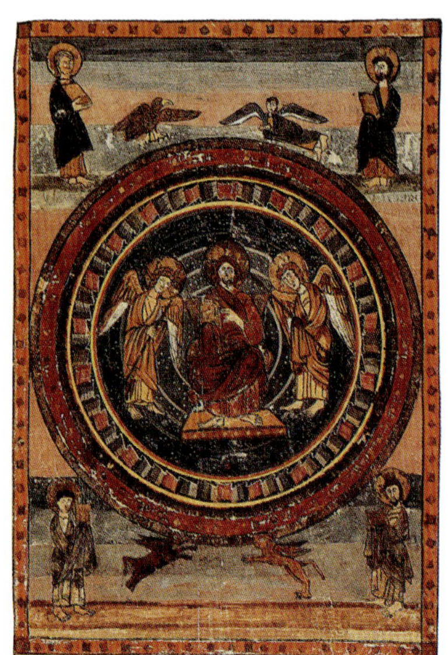

Opposite Terracotta horse's head, Japan, 6th century. (British Museum, OA, 1958, 050 7.1)

Opposite below left The Codex Amiatinus. Christ in Majesty, from one of the Bibles commissioned by Abbot Ceolfrith from the Wearmouth/Jarrow scriptorium, before 716. (Florence, Biblioteca Medicea-Laurenziana, MS Amiatino 1, f. 796v)

Opposite below right Clay plaque showing Buddha and attendants, Japan, 6th-7th century. The design recalls the Christian imagery of Christ in Majesty and may share a legacy from the art of Graeco-Roman antiquity or India. (British Museum, OA 1922, 1218.1)

Right Byzantine silk with riders, inscribed with the name Zachariou, 6th century. Silk production was copied from China and was greatly prized. (British Museum, MME 1904, 7-6,41)

Below Carpet pages from a small, portable Qur'an, made in Iraq in 1036. Such features may, like those in Insular art, have derived from earlier Coptic Egypt and the Middle East. (The British Library, APA Add. MS 7214, ff. 1v-2r)

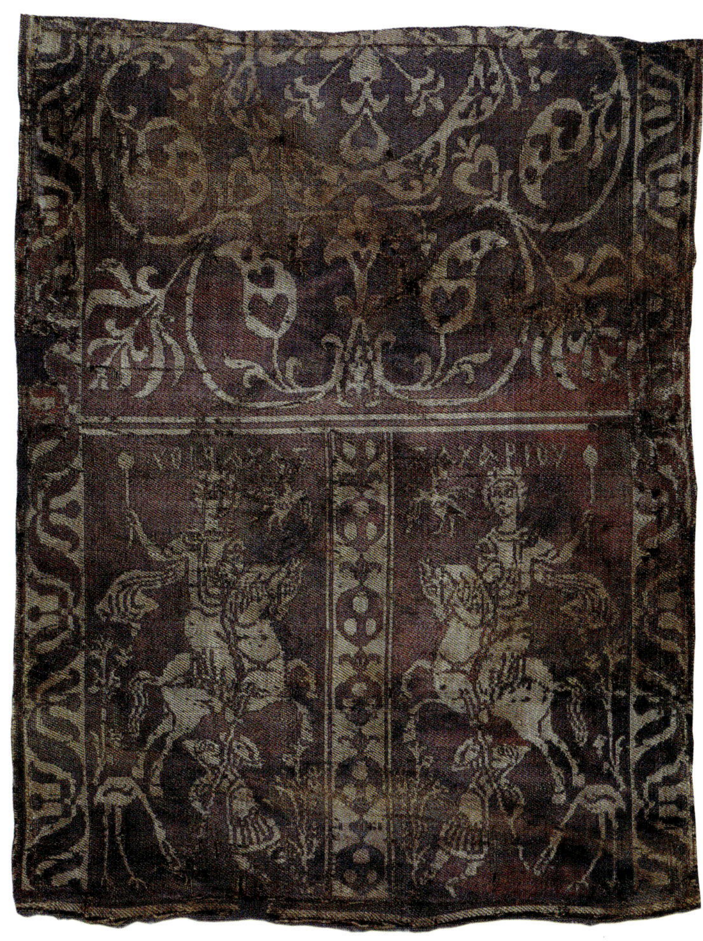

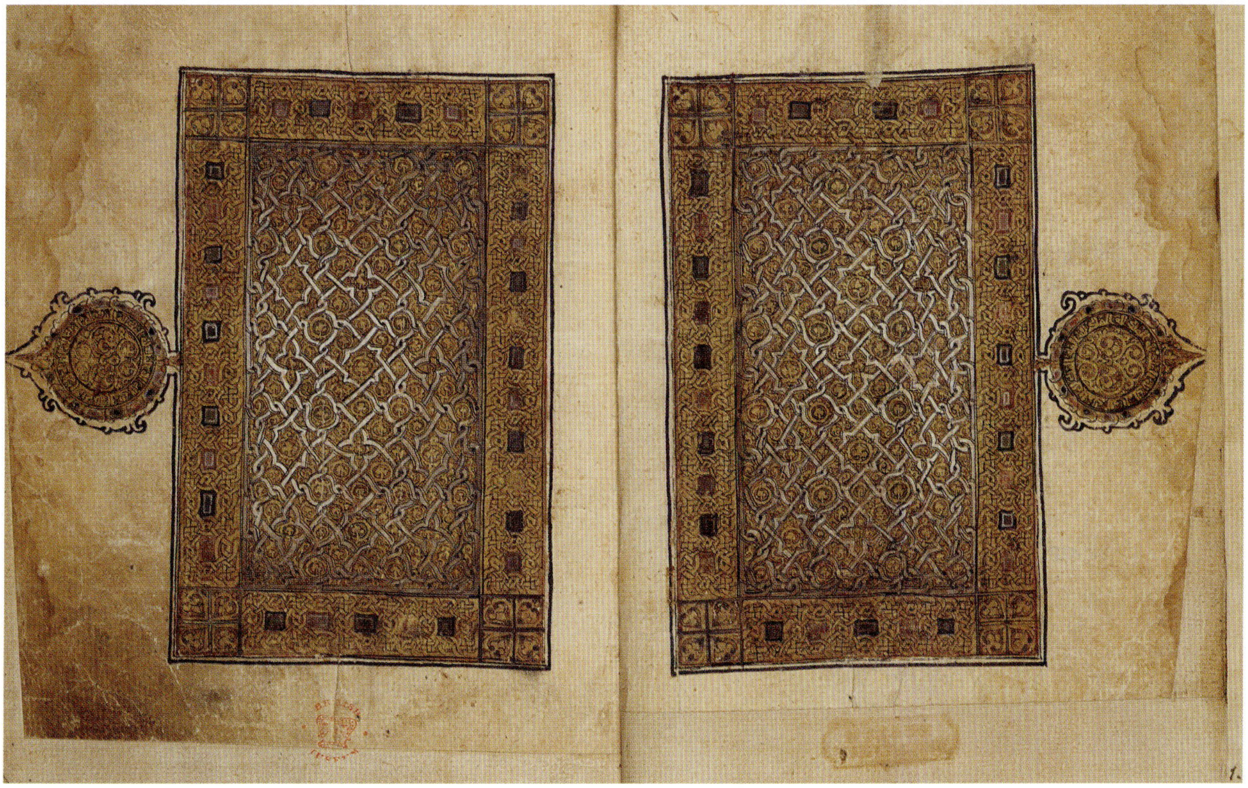

THE MEANING OF THE LINDISFARNE GOSPELS

What Did the Lindisfarne Gospels Mean to Their Makers?

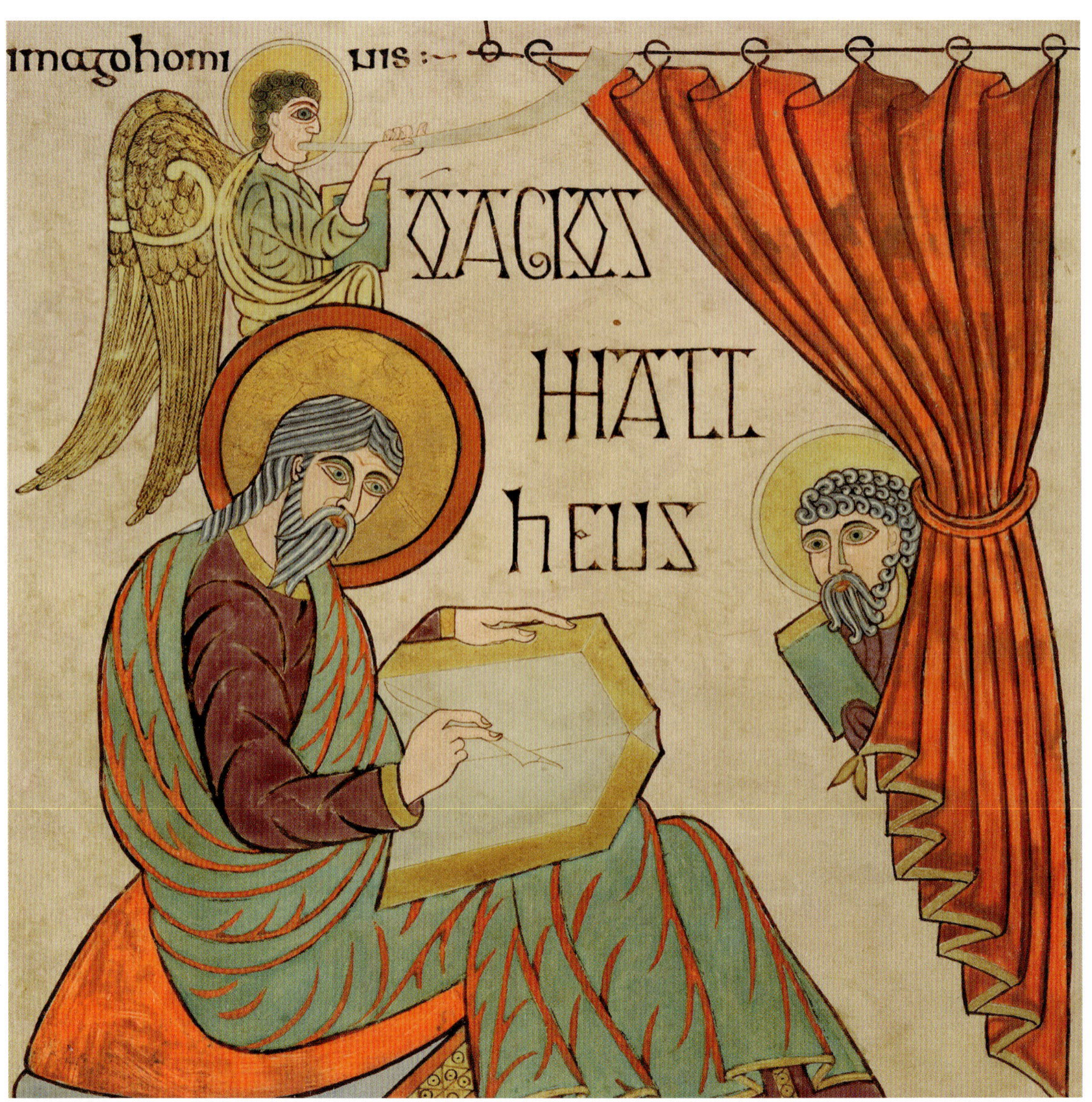

Above The scribe at work. Detail of the St Matthew miniature from the Lindisfarne Gospels, depicting the source of his inspiration. (The British Library, Cotton MS Nero D.iv, f. 25v)

Opposite Matthew evangelist miniature and incipit page from an Armenian Gospelbook produced at the monastery of Drazark, 1282. Armenia possessed one of the earliest Christian cultures, and later books such as this may have copied earlier ones. The scribe's tools are depicted in detail and he is inspired by his symbol (Matthew – the man) in the form of an angel. (The British Library, APA Or. MS 5626, ff. 1v-2r)

The scribe could become a channel between God and humanity, like the evangelists. Writing and painting sacred texts were absorbing acts of meditation, during which the scribe might glimpse the divine. Our artist-scribe undertook his physically and intellectually demanding labours on behalf of all Creation as a hermit, the book becoming his 'desert', like Christ in the wilderness and Cuthbert on Inner Farne. Cassiodorus said that each word written was a wound on Satan's body. This was the spiritual front-line.

Transmitting biblical texts was a high calling. Jerome's Vulgate version did not automatically supplant others already in circulation, with different versions often being compared, and it was nearly a thousand years until 'authorised' versions were published, such as the King James Bible. Aldred was not persecuted, like Wycliffe and Tyndale were later, for translating the Bible into English. The Anglo-Saxons wanted to spread the 'Good News' (*Godspell* – the Old English origin of the word 'Gospel').

What must it have been like to undertake the eye-straining, back-aching task of making such a book by hand in a hut on an island in the wild North Sea? Scribes occasionally noted that it was too cold to write. Monks attended eight church services each day and night, displayed humility by manual labour, prayed and studied. If our artist-scribe was also the Bishop he carried a heavy administrative burden, overseeing the spiritual and humanitarian needs of much of northern England and southern Scotland. Dedicating so much time suggests he saw it as his 'opus dei' (work for God). It would have taken him at least five years to complete.

This was a book to be seen, a shrine of sacred text and its role in the public prayer-life of the Church (the liturgy), and a cult focus. It would have been seen on the high altars of Lindisfarne, Chester-le-Street and Durham and used during important services. The monks had access, and guests were probably shown it. Ordinary people would have been able to see it, from a suitable distance, as pilgrims to the shrine. Glimpsing its mysteriously lit pages or covers could change their lives, such relics being famed for their powers of healing body and soul. It symbolised hope and a foretaste of a more beautiful existence to come.

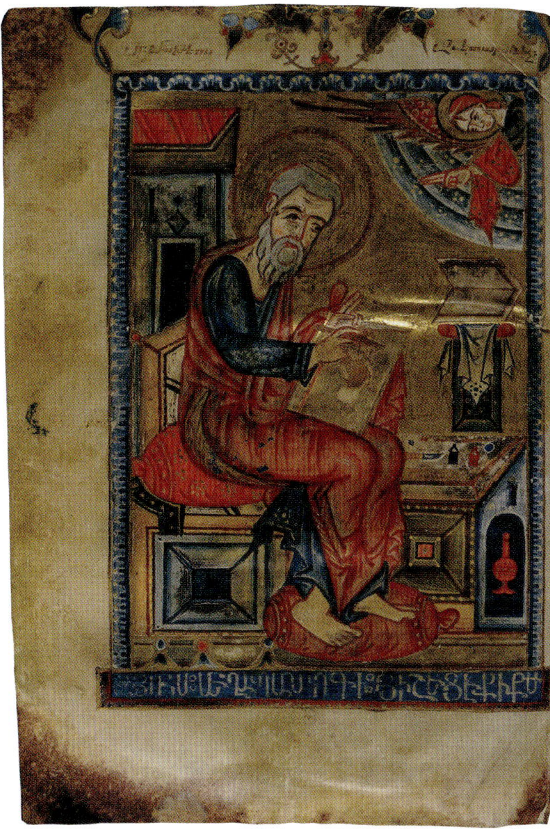

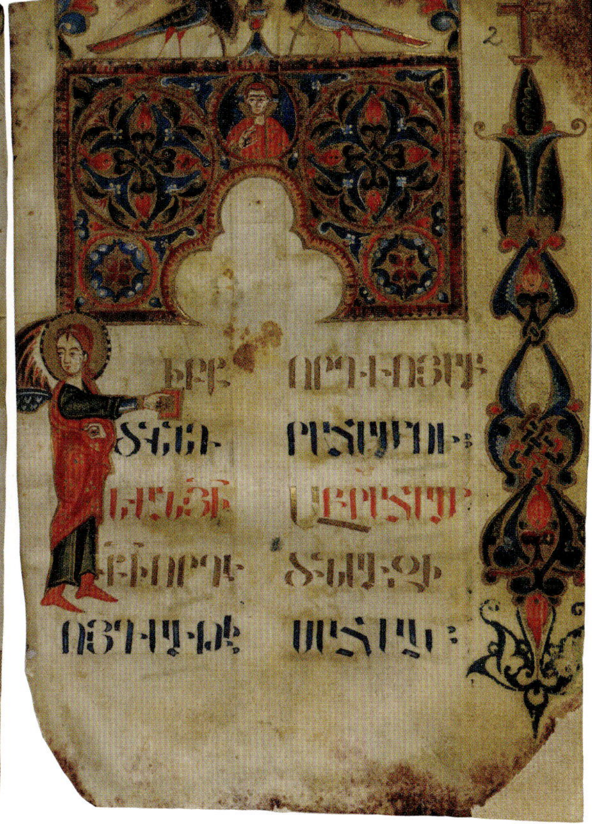

What Did the Lindisfarne Gospels Mean to Society?

The Anglo-Saxon kingdoms were governed by kings and nobles and, locally, by thegns and the thingemoot (folk meeting). Women enjoyed greater rights than their contemporaries elsewhere in Christendom, as well as in Judaism, Islam and the Graeco-Roman past. Anglo-Saxon women ran estates, nunneries and even double monasteries of monks and nuns, were adventurous missionaries and made books. Birth and/or property determined status. Slavery featured in all early societies, but the Church began working to abolish it. Kings and queens sometimes abdicated to become monks or nuns (or were forced to do so). One had to go back into battle – but carried only a wooden cross. Christianity certainly helped to transform Anglo-Saxon society, but also preserved its traditions.

Anglo-Saxon society and its rulers quickly saw the benefits of possessing an educated civil service and international diplomatic network, in the form of the Church. Celtic-style monasteries such as Lindisfarne also served as open-prisons for those doing penance and community service. Lay families attached themselves to live God-centered lives together and priests could be married, although celibacy was considered ideal. The Church produced written law-codes, genealogies establishing dynasties' legitimacy, and documents recording property transfers. They also became the repositories of group memory (epics such as 'Beowulf' being written down in the cloister) and of learning.

The Lindisfarne Gospels display their vision of Christianity in a manner that was designed to be welcoming to all, emphasising that this new culture stretched from Britain and Ireland to the farthest shores of the Mediterranean and was related to other faith traditions. Gregory the Great had again set the tone when he instructed Augustine to adopt the pagan shrines and festivals he encountered and transform them into Christian focuses.

You could tell a Pict, a Copt, a Frank, an Angle or a Saxon by their appearance. Dress and jewellery could be used to signal identity, belief and status in well-recognised ways. We often do the same today. Visual references made statements. The Lindisfarne Gospels, the Lindisfarne name-stones, the Ruthwell Cross and the Franks Casket combine Roman capitals and Germanic runes. The Anglo-Saxons were proclaiming themselves as heirs to Rome, while asserting their own new identity.

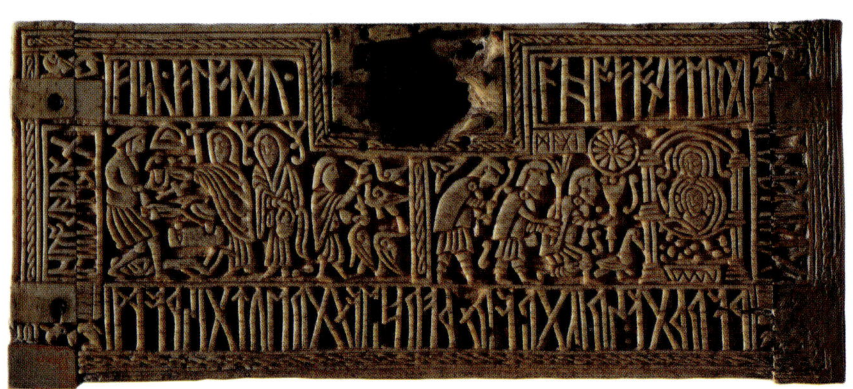

Left **The Franks Casket, a whalebone casket, perhaps a reliquary. Shown here is the front panel depicting Weyland the Smith (left) and the Adoration of the Magi (right), Northumbrian, 8th century. The scenes are drawn from world history and mythology and are identified by inscriptions in runes. Like Bede's** *History* **and the Lindisfarne Gospels it celebrates earlier cultures and assimilates them into a Christian present. (British Museum, MME 1867, 1-20, 1)**

What Do the Lindisfarne Gospels Mean Now?

The Lindisfarne Gospels are a greatly respected link with the beginnings of Christianity in the West. Outside of a faith context, many people see such witnesses to the past as valuable clues to their identities. The experience of the past can help us to question the present and inform the future. In the modern West we tend to compartmentalise life. Beliefs are often considered apart from ordinary life. This is counter to the teaching of most faiths. An uncompromisingly secular approach can lead to a lack of understanding of other people in the present, as well as of the past, and can hinder constructive relationships with other cultures.

How can we understand what motivated Cuthbert and Eadfrith? We create heroes, role models who can help us to live better lives – Gandhi, Nelson Mandela, Mother Theresa. We respect movements to help those in need – 'LiveAid' and 'Children in Need'. Cuthbert stood for something similar, providing aid, hope and working for social justice. He understood the dangers of basing society on materialism. Feeding the body alone was not enough. What mattered was feeding the spirit and achieving unity and harmony with all Creation and its maker. The Lindisfarne Gospels remain an eloquent testimony to such aspirations.

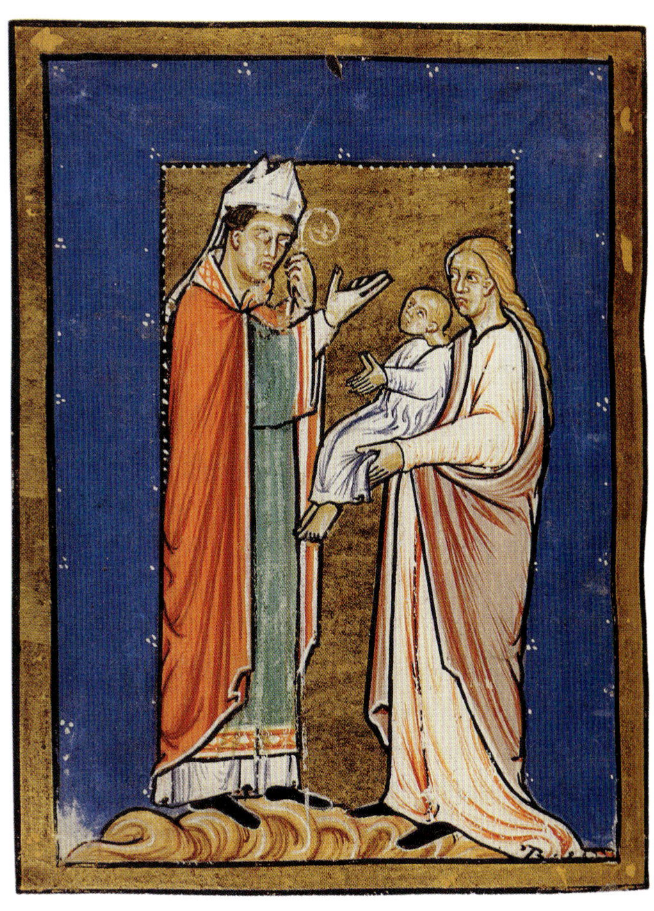

Opposite **Osgyth name-stone, marking the burial of a woman in the vicinity of Lindisfarne monastery, 7th-8th century. The name is given in runes (above) and roman capitals, resembling the display script in the Lindisfarne Gospels. (Lindisfarne Priory Museum, English Heritage)**

Above right **St Cuthbert heals a child, from an illustrated copy of Bede's** *Life of St Cuthbert,* **made at Durham in the late 12th century. Competition with the cult of Thomas Becket at Canterbury led the monks of Durham to remodel their later version of the cult of St Cuthbert to make it more attractive to female pilgrims. (The British Library, Yates Thompson MS 26, f.62v)**

Right **King David shown as an Anglo-Saxon King; opening of Psalm 26 of the The Vespasian Psalter, with 'historiated' (story-telling) initial 'D' depicting David and Jonathan, Kent, c.720-30. (The British Library, Cotton MS Vesp. A.i, ff. 30v-31r)**

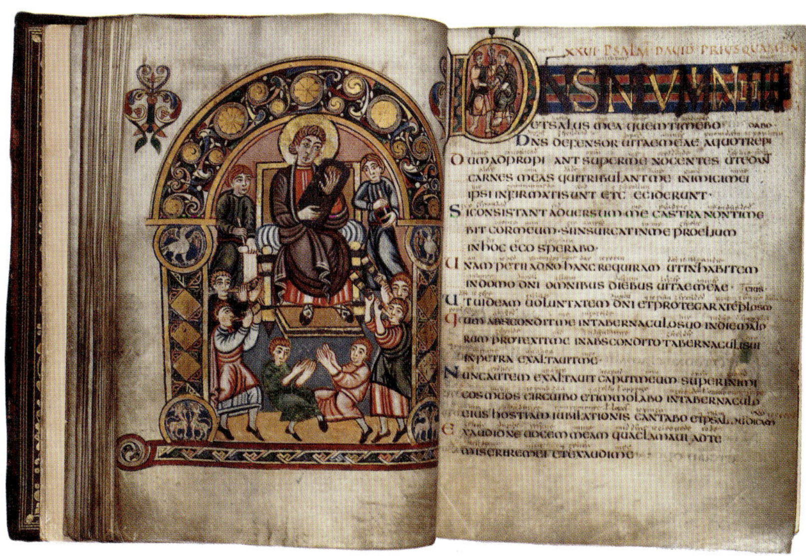

FURTHER READING

J. J. G. Alexander, *Insular Manuscripts, 6th to the 9th Century*, London, 1978

G. Bonner, *et al*, eds, *St Cuthbert, His Cult and His Community to AD 1200*, Woodbridge, 1989

M. P. Brown, *Anglo-Saxon Manuscripts*, London, 1991

M. P. Brown, *Understanding Illuminated Manuscripts. A Guide to Technical Terms*, Malibu and London, 1994

M. P. Brown, *The British Library Guide to Writing and Scripts*, London, 1998

M. P. Brown, *The Lindisfarne Gospels: Society, Spirituality and the Scribe*, London and Toronto, 2003

D. Buckton, *Byzantium. Treasures of Byzantine Art and Culture*, London, 1994

J. Campbell, *The Anglo-Saxons*, Oxford, 1982

K. Crossley-Holland, *The Anglo-Saxon World, an Anthology*, Oxford, 1982

Edwards, T. M. Charles, *Early Christian Ireland*, Cambridge, 2000

D. H. Farmer, ed., *The Age of Bede*, revd edn, Harmondsworth, 1983

D. H. Farmer, ed., Bede, *Ecclesiastical History of the English People*, London, 1990

D. Greene and F. O'Connor, eds, *A Golden Treasury of Irish Poetry AD 600-1200*, Dingle, 1967

G. Henderson, *From Durrow to Kells, the Insular Gospel-books 650-800*, London, 1987

F. Henry, *Irish Art in the Early Christian Period*, London, 1965

N. J. Higham, *The Kingdom of Northumbria*, Stroud, 1993

J. Leclercq, *The Love of Learning and the Desire for God*, New York, 1961

D. Marner, *St Cuthbert, His Life and Cult in Medieval Durham*, London, 2001

H. Mayr-Harting, *The Coming of Christianity to Anglo-Saxon England*, London, 1972

C. Nordenfalk, *Celtic and Anglo-Saxon Painting*, London, 1977

D. O'Sullivan and R. Young, *English Heritage Book of Lindisfarne, Holy Island*, London, 1995

M. Ryan, ed., *Treasures of Ireland. Irish Art, 3000 B.C.-1500 A.D.*, Dublin, 1983

P. Sheldrake, *Living Between Worlds. Place and Journey in Celtic Spirituality*, London, 1995

L. Webster and J. M. Backhouse, eds, *The Making of England: Anglo-Saxon Art and Culture AD 600-900*, London, 1991

K. Weitzmann, *Late Antique and Early Christian Book Illumination*, London, 1977

K. Wessel, *Coptic Art*, London, 1965

D. Whitelock, ed., *English Historical Documents* I, revd edn, London, 1979

D. M. Wilson, *Anglo-Saxon Art*, London, 1984

S. Youngs, ed., *'The Work of Angels', Masterpieces of Celtic Metalwork, 6th-9th Centuries AD*, London and Austin, 1989

THE NEW FACSIMILE

If the original manuscript was handled or moved too much it would not survive for future generations. A new facsimile produced by the British Library and Faksimile Verlag, Lucerne, means that more people can explore it in detail than at any other time in its history. The new facsimile is a state-of-the-art replica of the whole volume. Copies have been presented to Durham Cathedral and to the community Heritage Centre at Lindisfarne. Other copies will be found in major libraries and collections around the world. This gives more people the same level of access to this unique and fragile book as that given to scholars visiting the British Library reading rooms.

LIST OF EXHIBITS
British Library

Western MSS

Add. 5111, ff 10v-11r, Golden canon tables, Constantinople, *c*.600

Add. 5463, ff 3v-4r, Beneventan Gospels, canon tables, Benevento, mid-8th cent.

Add. 9381 Bodmin Gospels, wooden binding, 9th-10th cent.

Add. 10546, ff 25v-26r, Moutier Grandval Bible, Tours, *c*.830

Add. 11283, ff 2v-3r, Bestiary with transfer prickings, English, 12th cent.

Add. 11848 Carolingian Treasure Binding, Gospels, Tours early 9th cent.

Add. 21215, flyleaf and f.1r, Cassiodorus, Expositio in Psalterum, Carolingian late 8th cent.

Add. 22635, ff 44v-45r, Bede, *De locis sanctis*, 14th cent.

Add. 30850, ff 5v-6r, Mozarabic Antiphoner, Spanish, 11th cent.

Add. 34186 a, school exercise book, Lower Egypt, late 1st cent. (wax tablets)

Add. 35110, ff 97v-98r, Adomnán's *Life of St Columba*, Durham, late 12th cent.

Add. 37777 and 45025, ff.2v-3r, Ceolfrith Bible leaves, Wearmouth / Jarrow, Northumbria, before 716

Add. 38817, ff 1v-2r, Bede, *De Tabernaculo*, English, 12th cent.

Add. 40618, ff 22v-23r, Irish Pocket Gospels, S. Ireland, second half of 8th cent.

Add. 46204, verso, Worcester charter from Ceolfrith Bible, Worcester, 2nd half of 11th cent.

Add. 47967, flyleaf and f.1r, Helmingham Orosius flyleaf drawings, English, 10th cent.

Cot. Aug. II.2, uncial, earliest English charter, Hlothere of Kent to Reculver, 679

Cot. Claudius B.iv, ff 72v-73r, Aelfric Hexateuch, Canterbury, early 11th cent.

Cot. Domitian A.vii, ff 17v-18r, Durham Liber Vitae, Lindisfarne or Norham?, *c*.840

Cot. Nero D.iv, Lindisfarne Gospels, Lindisfarne, Northumbria, *c*.715-20

Cot. Otho B.vi, frag. 4, leaf from the Cotton Genesis, E. Mediterranean or Egypt, Alexandria?, *c*.500

Cot. Otho C.v, Cambridge-London Gospels, Northumbria, second quarter of 8th cent.

Cot. Tib A.xiv, ff 50v-51r, Bede, *Historia Ecclesiastica*, Wearmouth / Jarrow, mid-8th cent.

Cot. Tib. B.v, pt I, f.56v, Anglo-Saxon world map, Canterbury?, early 11th cent.

Cot. Tib. C.ii, ff 5v-6r, Bede, *Historia Ecclesiastica*, Canterbury, early 9th cent.

Cot. Titus A.ii, ff 29v-30r, Durham anthology with Cotton's note about the Lindisfarne Gospels

Cot. Titus C.xv, ff 2v-3r, Codex Purpureus Petropolitanus, Asia Minor or Syria, 6th cent.

Cot. Vesp. A.i, ff 30v-31r, Vespasian Psalter, Kent, Canterbury, *c*.720-30, Old English gloss mid-9th cent.

Cot. Vesp. B.vi, f.109r, episcopal lists, incl. Lindisfarne, and Northumbrian royal pedigrees, from the Anglian Collection, Mercia 805-814

Cot. Vesp. D.vi, ff 83v-84r, Stephanus, *Life of St Wilfrid*, English, 11th cent.

Eg. 617, ff 80v-81r, Wycliffe Bible owned by Thomas of Woodstock, English, 15th cent.

Hl 208, ff 10v-11r, Alcuin correspondence concerning Viking attacks, letter to Cudrado, f.11r

Hl 603 Harley Psalter, ff 17v-18r, Canterbury, early 11th cent.

Hl 1775, ff 223v-224r uncial Gospels, Italy, *c*.600

Hl 1802, ff 86v-87r, Armagh Gospels, Armagh, 1138

Hl 2506, ff 38v-39r, Cicero, Aratea, Fleury, with drawings by an Anglo-Saxon artist, late 10th cent.

Hl 2790, ff 27v-28r, Gedeon Gospels, Tours, *c*.796-804

Hl 2965, Book of Nunnaminster, Mercian prayerbook, W. Midlands, early 9th cent.

Hl 6018, ff 119v-120r, Cotton catalogue, partly in Cotton's own hand, 1621, including the Lindisfarne Gospels entry, f. 119v

Loan MS 74, binding, St Cuthbert Gospel (formerly Stonyhurst Gospel), Wearmouth / Jarrow, late 7th cent.

Loan MS 81, verso, Bankes Leaf from Ceolfrith Bible, Wearmouth / Jarrow, before 716

Royal 1.A.xiv, ff 171v-172r, Wessex Gospels, English, early 12th cent.

Royal 1.B.vii, ff 15v-16r, Northumbrian Gospels, Northumbria, second quarter of 8th cent.

Royal 1.B.ix, ff 4v-5r, transcript of part of the Lindisfarne Gospels gloss, 16th-17th cent.

Royal 1.E.vi, ff 4v-5r, Royal Bible, Canterbury, c.820-40

Royal 2.A.xx, ff 16v-17r, Mercian prayerbook focusing on medicine, W. Midlands, early 9th cent.

Royal 7.D.xxiv, ff 85v-86, Aldhelm, *De virginitate*, drawing, English, early 10th cent.

Royal 13.A.xi, Bede, *De Temporum Ratione*, English, early 12th cent.

Stowe 1061, ff 43v-44r, handmade facsimile compiled by T. Astle, English, 18th cent.

Yates Thompson 26, ff 62v-63 , *Life of St Cuthbert*, Durham, late 12th cent.

MS Facs 2043, Book of Kells facsimile, ed. P. Fox, *The Book of Kells* (1990), John incipit

MS Facs 630/1-2, Book of Durrow facsimile, ed. A. Luce *et al.*, *Evangeliorum quattuor Codex Durmachensis* (1960), John incipit

BL, APA collections

Or. 6799, ff 1v-2r, Dialogue on the Cross by Cyril of Jerusalem, Coptic Egypt, 10th cent.

Or. 4945, ff 2v-3r, Qur'an, Mosul, Iraq, 1310

Add. 7214, ff 1v-2r, Qur'an, Iraq, 1036

Or. 1347, ff 2v-3r, Taquinas, astrological table, 13th cent.

Or. 81, ff 111v-112r, Armenian Gospelbook, T'oros, monastery of Drazark, 1181-2

Or. 5626, ff 1v-2r, Armenian Gospelbook, monastery of Drazark, 1282

Or. 4445, ff 80v-81r, Hebrew Bible with Masorah, Middle East, 10th cent.

Or. 2628, ff 184v-185r, Hebrew Bible, Lisbon, Portugal, 1483, carpet page with micrography

Or.59.bb.5, frontispiece, *Nihon Shoki*, History of Japan

Or. 8210 / S.6983, early example of Chinese paper

Or. 8210 / P.19, early example of Chinese printing

Or. 78.a.11, Million charms of Empress Shotoku, printed, Japan, Nara, AD761-70

BL, Printed Collections

G.2216 Joseph Strutt, *Horda Angel-cynnan; or a Compleat View of the Manners, Customs, Arms, Habits, Etc. of the inhabitants of England*, 3 vols (1775-6), III, pls XXIII-XXVI

External loans

Durham Cathedral

Durham A.ii.17, f.38³v-38⁴r, The Durham Gospels, Lindisfarne or daughter-house, *c*.700

Durham A.ii.10, ff 3v-4r, Gospelbook, Northumbria, 7th-cent.

Durham A.iv.19 The Durham Ritual, with Aldred gloss, Wessex, 10th cent. (*c*.970)

Replica of St Cuthbert's pectoral cross, original 7th cent.

Sculpture 8 Hexham wall slab with archer, late 7th cent.

Sculpture 20 Cross head with Last Judgement and Baptism, Durham, 11th cent.

Sculpture 24 Durham grave cover, 10th-11th cent.

Sculpture 28 Hartlepool name-stone (Berehtgy), *c*.700

Jarrow, St Paul's Church

Sculpture, 'in hoc signum' cross, late 7th cent.

Sculpture, inhabited vinescroll with birds, late 7th cent.

Stone baluster shaft, late 7th cent.

Monkwearmouth, St Peter's Church (Durham Diocese)

Sculpture no. 4, fragment from altar screen with animal interlace, late 7th cent.

Baluster shaft, late 7th cent.

Chester-le-Street, Church of St Mary and St Cuthbert

Eadmund cross-shaft, early 10th cent.

English Heritage, Holy Island, Lindisfarne Priory Museum

81077015 Osgyth name-stone, *c*.700

81077019 Beanna name-stone, *c*.700

81077017 name-stone with interlace terminals, *c*.700

81077047 cross shaft with animal interlace, 9th cent.

81077057 gravemarker with 'Viking horde' symbolising Last Judgement, 9th cent.

81077065 cross shaft with Christ and evangelists, 9th-10th cent.

Lichfield Cathedral, Dean and Chapter

MS s.n., pp.220-221, The Lichfield Gospels, Northumbria?, mid-8th cent.

Cambridge, Corpus Christi College

MS 197B, ff 1v-2r, Cambridge-London Gospels, Northumbria, second quarter 8th cent.

British Museum
Medieval and Modern European

2002. 5-2, 1, Bird stud, Freckenham, Suffolk

1982, 10-2, Byzantine cross with Virgin and evangelists, 6th cent.

Inv 25a Sutton Hoo, three recently excavated harness mounts with zoomorphic interlace, early 7th cent.

1916.7-5.1 Steeple Bumpstead boss, Irish, 8th cent.

1811, 12-14,1 Asgarsby, Lincs., cruciform brooch to show 'ethnic' dress forms

1867, 2-4,6 Frilford, Berks., saucer brooch to show 'ethnic' dress forms

1905, 4-18.16 Wickhambreux stud, Kent, 7th cent

1097'70, Gibbs Collection, Faversham buckle, Anglo-Saxon, early 7th cent

1851, 10-11,7, Caenby mount, Lincs., Anglo-Saxon, early 7th cent.

996, 7-1,1 replica of Franks Casket, Northumbria, early 8th cent.

1824, ring 5 Gold ring with sacred monogram, Byzantine, 6th cent.

1860, 10-2,46 Pottery lamp with birds, Carthage, c.440-550

1904, 7-6,41 Byzantine silk with horsemen, inscribed 'Zachariou', 6th cent.

1883,8-8,1 Byzantine pilgrim's ampulla with evangelist, Asia Minor, 550-650

1866,12-11,3 Coin weight with monogram found in Somerset (possibly from an Anglo-Saxon burial), Constantinople? 6th cent.

1986,4-6,18 Justinian I glass weight with bilingual Greek/Latin inscription, Constantinople? 527-565

1987, 12-3,1, Lombardic silver cross, 7th cent.

Inv.26 b, c, Two anthropomorphic strap ends

1902, 3-15, 1, Bone leaf from a wax tablet, Blythburgh, Anglo-Saxon, 8th cent.

BM, Dept of Coins and Medals

1971, 12-16-52 Penny (sceat), Continental Series E, 'Porcupine' type (VOIC group), Frisia, *c*.700-710

1860, 12-31-7 Dinar of the 'Abbasid Caliph al-Mansur, AD 773/4

Keany catalogue 115. Series U, bird-in-vine

1896, 4-4-15. Coin of Pada with runic inscription

1913, 12-13-1 Dinar / mancus of Offa of Mercia, AD 773/4, copying Islamic coin

1921,12-13-1 Type 48, whorl of heads, Anglo-Saxon, 7th cent.

1850,3-6-10 Type 34, Celtic cross, Anglo-Saxon, 7th cent.

1982, 7-38-11 Type 35, long-legged bird, Anglo-Saxon, 7th cent.

1854,6-12-23 coin of King Aldfrith of Northumbria, with lion, late 7th cent.

BM Oriental Antiquities
BM Chinese

1936.10.12.43, court lady with pigmentation, 8th cent.

1910.6.14.1, funerary jar with dragon handles, 7th-8th cent.

BM Japanese

1958.0507.1 Earthenware haniwa figure of horse's head

OA 1255 Bronze horse bit

1922, 1218.1 and 1922, 1218.15 Two depictions of Buddha, one flanked by female worshippers, the other a smaller seated figure

1936, 1118.136 Gilt bronze annular sword pommel with the head of a phoenix

1954, 1021.1 Wood gigaku mask of Shishiko

BM Egyptian (Coptic)

21518 textile with bird and vases, Egypt, 5th-7th cent.

18219 textile with lion and tree border on linen, Egypt, 5th-7th cent.

18236 textile with hare and vases with interlace, Egypt, 5th-7th cent.

17082 Pilgrim's ampulla with St Menas and camels, Abu Mena, Egypt, 6th cent.

59743 Metalwork relic cross with Virgin and Child and censing angels, Egypt, 6th cent.

71890 Nubian processional wooden cross, 7th-14th cent.

618 Stella with eagle, vinescroll, interlace and cross, Egypt, 6th-7th cent.

1801 Arched headstone with paired birds and beasts beneath interlaced arcade and tabula ansata inscription, Egypt, 6th-7th cent.

1611 Inhabited vinescroll with grape-pickers, Egypt, 6th cent.

69035 Cross slab, Egypt, 6th-7th cent.

BM Islamic

Brook Sewell Fund 1959.10-23.1 Brass ewer with foliate scrolls and senmurv, Iran, 8th-9th cent.

Franks Bequest 1897, 1963.12-103 Silver gilt dish with feasting prince, Mazandaran, Iran, 7th-8th cent.

1981.3-5.1 Silver gilt repoussé bowl with marigolds and central 'cross', Iran, 8th-9th cent.

OA+10618-19/10621-3. Three plaster frescoes, human heads and goose, baths of the harem of the Jawsaq al-Khaqani at Samarra, Iraq, 8th-9th cent.

1973.6-23.1 Boss of mosaic glass, Iraq, 9th cent.

A.18-1929 Bone handle with ibis and vase, Egypt, 9th-10th cent.

1964.7-13.1 Bowl with stylised figure, monochrome lustre over cream glaze, Iraq, 9th-10th cent.

V&A Museum

Medieval Antiquities Dept, Inv. No. 254-1867 Anglo-Saxon-style Continental ivory, 8th cent.

Metalwork Dept., Replicas of Tara brooch and Ardagh Chalice (Nat. Mus. Ireland), Irish, 8th cent.

Sculpture Collection, 4312-1856 Mosaic head of Christ, S.Michele in Africisco, Ravenna, c.545

Science Museum, London

1983-1393 Portable sundial and calendar, Constantinople? c.500

National Museums of Scotland, Edinburgh

NMS FC269 St Ninian's Isle bowl, Pictish, 8th cent.

NMS FC9 Dunbeath penannular brooch fragment, Scottish in Irish style, 8th cent.

NMS FC5 Isle of Mull penannular brooch, 8th cent.

GP 219 Dunadd 'in nomine' inscribed pebble, 7th or 8th cent.

RMS GP 218, Dunadd brooch motif piece, Irish style 8th-9th cent.

IB 298 Aberlady cross shaft, Northumbrian (near Edinburgh), 8th cent.

IB 286 Inscribed stone, Tarbat, Pictish / Columban, 8th cent.

IB 335 Cast of Dunfallandy Stone, Pictish, 8th-9th cent.

IB 127 Rosemarkie Daniel Pictish Sculpture

Historic Scotland

DA 653 Dunadd brooch mould, 7th cent.

Jedburgh Abbey, sculptured slab from a screen, Anglo-Saxon, 8th to early 9th cent. (cast)

National Museums Liverpool

Inv. No. M 6226 Kingston Down brooch, Anglo-Saxon, early 7th cent.

1966.155.1 Fragment of limestone frieze depicting lion in vine-scroll, Egypt, 5th-6th cent.

Inv. No. M7013-M7020 St Martin's Canterbury hoard, b, Kentish 'medalet' of Bishop Liudhard, late 6th cent.

Ulster Museum

A3.1991 Clonmore shrine, Irish, 7th cent.

A17259 shrine mount, Irish, 7th-8th cent.

Deerparks Farm stud and motif piece, Irish, 7th-8th cent.

National Museum of Ireland, Dublin

NMI 1986:141 Lough Kinale book shrine, Irish, late 8th cent.

NMI 1985:21,b,d,e Donore handle assembly, Irish 8th cent.

NMI R.4006 The Soiscél Molaise, Irish, late 8th-9th, 11th and 15th cent.

NMI P.782a, Petrie Collection, Openwork mount, Phoenix Park, Dublin, Irish, 8th cent.

NMI 1881:526a Bronze enamelled toilet implement, Irish, 5th-6th cent.

NMI E33: 1385 Dooey motif piece, Irish, 5th-6th cent.

NMI E.14:1572 a,b Lagore mould and stud, Irish, 8th cent.

NMI 1958:20 Lough Gara belt-buckle, Irish, 7th-8th cent.

NMI X.2981 Openwork mount with zoomorphic interlace, Irish, 8th cent.

NMI W3 Monasterevin bronze disc, Irish, 1st-2nd cent.

First published in 2003 by
The British Library
96 Euston Road
London NW1 2DB

British Library Cataloguing-in-Publication Data
A catalogue record for this book is available from The British Library

ISBN 0 7123 4811 5

Designed by The British Library Corporate Design Office
Printed in England by Balding + Mansell
Map by John Mitchell